AF607816

The Human Figure on Film

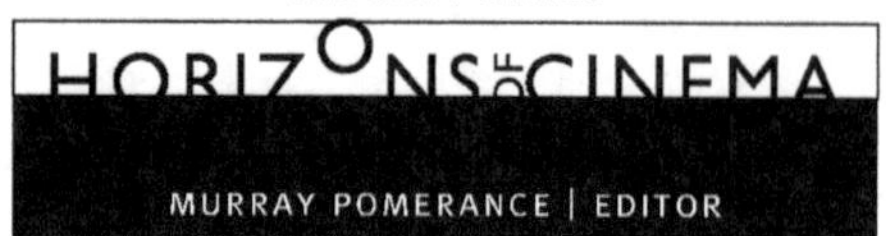

RECENT TITLES

Daniel Varndell, *Torturous Etiquettes*

Jonah Corne and Monika Vrečar, *Yiddish Cinema*

Jason Jacobs, *Reluctant Sleuths, True Detectives*

Lucy J. Miller, *Distancing Representations in Transgender Film*

Tomoyuki Sasaki, *Cinema of Discontent*

Mary Ann McDonald Carolan, *Orienting Italy*

Matthew Rukgaber, *Nietzsche in Hollywood*

David Venditto, *Whiteness at the End of the World*

Fareed Ben-Youssef, *No Jurisdiction*

Tony Tracy, *White Cottage, White House*

Tom Conley, *Action, Action, Action*

Lindsay Coleman and Roberto Schaefer, editors, *The Cinematographer's Voice*

Nolwenn Mingant, *Hollywood Films in North Africa and the Middle East*

†Charles Warren, edited by William Rothman and Joshua Schulze, *Writ on Water*

Jason Sperb, *The Hard Sell of Paradise*

William Rothman, *The Holiday in His Eye*

Brendan Hennessey, *Luchino Visconti and the Alchemy of Adaptation*

Alexander Sergeant, *Encountering the Impossible*

Erica Stein, *Seeing Symphonically*

George Toles, *Curtains of Light*

A complete listing of books in this series can be found online at www.sunypress.edu

The Human Figure on Film

Natural, Pictorial, Institutional, Fictional

Seth Barry Watter

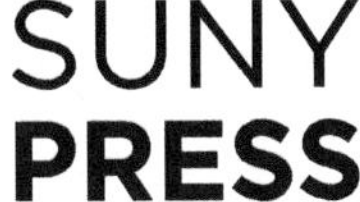

Cover image: *Microcultural Incidents in Ten Zoos*, dir. Ray L. Birdwhistell and Jacques D. Van Vlack, 1971. Courtesy of Joanne D. Birdwhistell, Jill R. Birdwhistell, Nan Birdwhistell, and Jason Birdwhistell Rothberg.

Published by State University of New York Press, Albany

Printed in the United States of America

For information, contact State University of New York Press, Albany, NY
www.sunypress.edu

Library of Congress Cataloging-in-Publication Data

Name: Watter, Seth Barry, 1987– author.
Title: The human figure on film : natural, pictorial, institutional, fictional / Seth Barry Watter.
Description: Albany : State University of New York Press, [2023] | Series: SUNY series, horizons of cinema | Includes bibliographical references and index.
Identifiers: LCCN 2022062260 | ISBN 9781438495088 (hardcover : alk. paper) | ISBN 9781438495101 (ebook)
Subjects: LCSH: Human body in motion pictures. | Digital cinematography.
Classification: LCC PN1995.9.B62 W38 2023 | DDC 791.43/653—dc23/eng/20230802
LC record available at https://lccn.loc.gov/2022062260

10 9 8 7 6 5 4 3 2 1

All of a sudden, I went to get a sheet of paper, carefully pointed a stick of charcoal and began to try outlining one limb and then another, then, as nothing much came of that, more swiftly to get the whole shape of the left arm up to the armpit, and the continuous motion from that point right along to the left side where the yielding was; but my hand was unpractised in this, and not until the charcoal had got a little blunt, would the line of itself grow more real and a certain life infuse itself into my fingers. But now it was the eye which was not accustomed, in dealing with the human figure, to flash its light quickly enough to the hand; I had to stand up and examine more precisely the boundaries and the transitions, and, moreover, because I was too old now to proceed in an unintelligent fashion, I had to meditate upon the things and their relation to one another.

—Gottfried Keller, *Der grüne Heinrich*

Contents

Illustrations

Preface

This is a book about people watching people. More specifically, it deals with dissimilar ways that people look at people. The people who are looked at happen to be on film, and a moment's introspection is probably enough to show us that we do not always see them in the same way. They change in appearance in accord with our interest. When a particular interest is made to dominate others, it becomes a methodology, asking questions it can answer. Hence, this book could be called a survey of methodologies. It is an attempt to sort out some of the concepts we use that are usually all mixed up when we watch films of people. But it is also about the difficulty of using just one concept.

I have called this book a survey; it is not a book of theory, if by that we mean a system of interlocking propositions. Rather, my approach is descriptive of how some people in the past have looked at other people. It is an attempt at historical reconstruction without, for all that, really being a book of history. The great advantage of using historical materials is that they are always more surprising than what we dream up. They show us how writers grappled with particular images. For film studies, anyway, this seems more instructive than trying to make sense of the crumbs the philosophers throw us.

In the interest of readability, I have largely confined quotations to primary sources. This may strike some as odd in an academic book but the Horizons of Cinema series aims to reach a wider than academic audience. Generally, only academics care about who is citing whom. Another way of putting it is that I have tried to apply the rule of Chekhov's gun to the present study. Readers are not given more or less than they need to know; unless it has dramatic relevance, any additional name is a source of extra friction. Of course some will want to know if I have "done my homework"; this is what the endnotes and acknowledgments are for.

Acknowledgments

Zeynep Çelik Alexander, Gianni Barchiesi, Noam Elcott, Eric Ehrhardt, Tanya Goldman, Byron Hamann, Gertrud Koch, Dominic Lash, Rochelle Sara Miller, Dana Polan, Stefanie Proksch-Weilguni, Ellen Rooney, Jakub Stejskal, George Toles, and Deborah Weinstein all read and gave feedback on material included here.

Martha Davis, Henning Engelke, Bernard Dionysius Geoghegan, the late Adam Kendon, Michael Lempert, Heather Love, and Adrian Martin deserve special thanks; as does Joel Simundich, who also prepared the index, although this is really the least of his contributions.

Mark Mahoney, Alex Pezzati, Kate Pourshariati, Mark White, Pam Wintle, and Kathryn Ramey rendered valuable archive assistance. My thanks to the Birdwhistell family and the Bateson Idea Group for permission to reproduce certain frame enlargements here.

Brian Wall stimulated early interest in the subject. Philip Rosen taught me much about the tough craft of writing when this book was a dissertation that he directed. Murray Pomerance helped me to eventually see it as, in fact, a book that might be published. Chris Conklin will always be my first teacher in film.

Some of these chapters appeared in earlier versions, although they have been heavily reworked in accord with our thematic focus. Chapter 1 draws on "Scrutinizing: Film and the Microanalysis of Behavior," *Grey Room*, no. 66 (2017): 32–69. Chapter 4 hews more closely to its source, "On the Concept of Setting: A Study of V. F. Perkins," *Journal of Cinema and Media Studies* 58, no. 3 (2019): 72–92. Many thanks to these journals for permission to reproduce portions here.

I completed the manuscript during a difficult time in the history of the world. I was lucky to have the support of a NOMIS postdoctoral fellowship from 2020 to 2021, which gave me an office and an intellectual community at the eikones Center of the University of Basel. Friederike Zenker, as director, made the stay a very nice one, and so did many others. I also thank the selection committee—Markus Klammer, Markus Krajewski, Malika Maskarinec, Lorenza Mondada, Ralph Ubl, and Markus Wild—for their initial vote of confidence.

Most important of all, of course, are Faith Holland and Hildegard "Hildy" Holland Watter.

Introduction

The Human Figure on Film

Few things hold the gaze as does the human figure. Movement in the figure holds the gaze even more. It is, at once, the most obvious and elusive of all our concerns. It is obvious because we see it in the course of daily life: on the street, out of windows, at work, in the mirror. We appraise and evaluate the figures of others; we act on the basis of the signs they give off. We draw close to ones whose movements are agreeable and avoid those that threaten some possible danger. Yet if called upon to give our criteria for judgment, we might balk and protest and soon be at a loss for words. "Why was it the movement of his arm stirred her as nothing else in the world could?" asks D. H. Lawrence.[1] The question goes unanswered; the movement remains elusive; and the figure that stands before us becomes an utter mystery. This is not, in itself, unpleasant or bad. A world without mystery would be a poor thing indeed. Still, one feels there are more pointed questions that could and should be asked of a thing of such great interest.

~

Whatever questions we pose are likely to arise as well when we see such figures moving on a screen, in a film. Almost all films are full of human figures that file past the camera "as though of right."[2] They are there in the early days, kissing and sneezing; soon they are living, loving, and dying; by the end of the 1920s they are even seen talking. Names like Vitascope and Biograph support the impression that life itself is on display when the figures start to move. The cinema might even function as a surrogate for life; the screen is full of energy and we leave the theater "charged." The prototype of such a naive response is given by Frank Norris in his novel *McTeague* (1899). "Look at that horse move his head," McTeague gasps. "Look at that cable car coming—and the man going across the street." Mrs. Sieppe beside him says she knows it is a trick; little Owgooste falls asleep as he struggles to hold his bladder. But McTeague remains riveted, "quite carried away," and each new image draws from him some further exclamation. Later, going home, he assesses the performance. "Wasn't—wasn't that magic lantern wonderful, where the figures moved? Wonderful—ah, wonderful!"[3] The whole episode is proof of the character's simplicity. Yet most of us today do not get much further. We might use more and bigger words, but the substance would be the same. Though we speak with conviction of this or that actor, of this or that performance as good or poor, we do not really know what provokes the impression and we fall back on language that convinces no one. The adjectives we use are curiously resistant to verbal expansion or extension of the referent. What remains are a perception—namely, that the figures moved—and a feeling wedded to it, such as "ah, wonderful!"

Wonderful is not always a bad place to start. It marks a thing of vital interest to the person who says it. And so one might begin with the work of description: of saying what is there as it changes or doesn't. Then one will at least have a more precise record of whatever it is that elicited wonder. Some films consist, or seem to consist, of little more than moments that make us feel wonder. *The Big Sleep* (1946), for instance, has been said to work this way. Its plot is hard to follow and it is best not to try. The film has other compensations; it is interesting to look at. Apparently its authors had no greater ambition than to make every sequence into "something that was fun."[4] My own favorite scene occurs fairly early when the hero first enters the house on Laverne Terrace. I see that figure enter after screaming and gunshots and a bright flash of light have caught its attention, and I am entranced. I see it run from a car across the darkened street and to the front door, then to a nearby window; kick the window open, step in and look around; investigate the setting, which includes a man and woman. The man is quite dead and the woman, intoxicated. In any case they are part of what functions as background. For one or two minutes there is just the mute poetry of a human figure as it moves against this background.

Poetry, of course, is not just ineffable. It has a material vehicle that can be analyzed quite prosaically. One can look at the image and make a plain description, which in our case would probably go something like this. Shot 1: Long shot of the windows from inside the house as the running man enters through them. The windows open at his kick and the score abruptly ceases. He steps down and looks around. A sofa flanks him on one side and a chair on the other. The camera pans slightly as he takes a few steps into the room and looks offscreen left. Shot 2: Long shot of a bedroom as seen through hanging beads, which sway gently with the wind coming in from the window. Shot 3: Medium shot of the entrant, who looks from offscreen left to offscreen right. Shot 4: Long shot of a woman sitting in a wooden chair, humming, using an index finger to stroke her left knee. She never looks up; at the end of the shot, she titters. The chair is in an alcove on a slightly raised platform with another couch behind it. In the setting there are statues, incense burners, embroidered drapery, and other things. Shot 5: The man walks through the room, eyes lowered and mostly covered by the shadow of a hat—and so on.

But this attempt at a plain description is not very successful. It has already made a number of assumptions about visible figures and units of analysis. For one, the figures are given genders: there is a man and there is a woman. They are distinguished as living from another figure who is dead. The film is broken down in terms of separate shots, or periods of apparently continuous shooting, and hence the observations are preponderantly macro, for they deal with units ranging from one to sixty seconds. Perhaps a more granular form of description would avoid the assumptions of everyday language. We could, for example, call the figures A and B, and then proceed to map their physical displacements at a frame-by-frame level, one limb at a time. We could say every time a given limb moves and in what direction it moves across the screen. We could mark every change of flexion to extension or from adduction to abduction in all movable parts, as well as note the scale of the figures in the frame and any displacements of the camera that frames them. We could, finally, look at all this as a train of events in time that also builds a space out of fragments of space. But we would not get any closer to a form of observation that makes no assumptions about what is seen. Our language betrays us. We still assume, for instance, that the figure is human; that the human has a figure; that a camera has framed it—framed it in unreal space. Thus any description of it is laden with concepts, if not with a fully formed theory about it. As soon as we take any step beyond "wonderful!" we are already working with one or more concepts. And each of these concepts can generate knowledge when pressed into service self-consciously, systematically.

If I think I am looking at a moving human figure, I inevitably ascribe to it the quality of life, and life, whatever else it may be, is sustained by interaction with its surroundings. It lives in a state of dynamic exchange with the flora and fauna of its environment. So when I see the running figure move over to the house, I see not mere motion but a response to the environment: in this case to the noise and the flash of bright light that decisively change the aspect of the environment. Let us call this a natural-historical way of looking, with a natural human organism as the object of our regard. We are interested in the relation of organism to environment and in the emergent quality of the organism's behavior. This particular organism, a fortyish white male, can be seen to behave differently before and after the commotion. Before he is slouching and dozing in a car as he puffs the last smoke from a stubby cigarette. After, his gaze becomes fixed on a definite object and his muscles contract in a new state of tension. Then he launches forward across the street and yard. The impulsion, however, is suddenly checked upon entry to the house through the French windows. His movements grow slower as if he now passes through a more viscous medium than the air outside; his eyes, blinking constantly, scan the room for evidence. Shifting our own gaze from region to region, we start to find patterns, regularities of behavior. We might see, for instance, that most of his movement is done in the regions of head and hands; even more specifically, around his mouth and fingers. The line of his shoulders almost never changes as he walks, and his arms always seem to be slightly akimbo. The majority of his figure holds together as a block, which makes the small flurries in head and hands that much clearer. Whenever something puzzles him he does one of two things: exposes the teeth slightly or taps with his fingers. He does this with the corpse, the cocktail, and a hollow head of Buddha with a camera inside it. He peers inside the head and grazes it with his fingers, then peers at its face and taps the table under it. Most of his movements are short and precise and clearly marked by pauses like the space between words. It would be difficult for us to notice them otherwise with all the competition offered by the decor.

For, whatever else the scene may be, it is also an affair of shapes. It impresses the viewer with a clash of different shapes, with the eccentric lines resulting from its overdressed aspect. The pan-Asian decor seems intended, at one level, to make a death inscrutable with hints of Eastern mystery. But at another level of reception, the inscrutableness results from the scattering of our gaze. Strong shapes at the periphery vie with the human figure, which is really just one shape among many others. Such is the effect, at any rate, of the pictorial mode of looking that I have adopted. I no longer see a woman sitting in a chair; I see a diagonal formed by the extended leg of a figure posed forty-five degrees to the camera. I see the twist of a dragon across the figure's sleeveless dress that echoes and is echoed by other forms in the vicinity: the shadows of tracery cast on the wall behind, the curling smoke that rises from a bulbous incense burner. All of which contributes to my impression that the woman is quite at home here, that her shape is congruent. The intruder, however, is decidedly not at home. His shape is incongruent with the shapes I see around it. Pausing before the curtains of the French windows, it falls into a space that rapidly narrows into the point of a triangle formed by two lines: one from the armchair to the figure's right, the other by a sofa to the figure's left. Moreover, our eyes may be pulled from this figure in the center to the extreme periphery because of a standing lamp, whose twisting form spans the frame from top to bottom. It, too, is shaped like a dragon, with dragon-shaped handles and curlicues of flame. The thing is so striking that even the camera seems affected when it tracks and swivels backward, tracing an S in space.

We may start to think that the man's constant blinking is due to the strain of this view on his eyes. Or perhaps it is due to the fatigue of the actor whose figure this is, the actor named Bogart. We know his name from the credits where "Humphrey Bogart" appears over a man's silhouette. We may have known it already from his appearance in other films. If so, then his appearance in this one becomes a phase of his persona and an entry in a list of all his screen credits. I realize that as I watch him, I watch him at work, and I happen to have a sense of how such work proceeds. Other films and shows have dramatized the process of making a film under similar conditions, and an enormous literature of memoirs, biographies, and reports has grown up around this social institution. When I take from the shelf a book about Bogart and follow the index entry for *The Big Sleep*, I come upon the following piece of information. "Bogart's personal turmoil dominated the production almost from its October 1944 shoot. On several days Bogart was late reporting for work"—a pattern that continued and intensified through November.[5] Not only was he late, but his acting also seemed to suffer; he resorted to old and half-forgotten tics. His marriage was breaking up in a very public way while he worked back to back on films the whole year. One wonders if the scene in the house on Laverne Terrace was filmed before or after he had his nervous breakdown; before or after the studio forced him out of bed to work. In any case his gestures start to look different when seen in the mode of institutional vision. They seem like the lazy protest of someone who, in his own words, was "tired of the studio's attitude that I am a half-witted child."[6] The image becomes a prison whose bars are the shadows cast by the arc lights just outside the frame.

These shadows are at once a part of the environment, an element of composition, and an index of filmmaking as an institution. They might also be expressive of a whole state of mind if I concede that the human figure does have a thing called *mind*. I would then treat the figure more or less as a character, in the sense that this word is normally used—as an individual with fears, goals, and desires, with feelings that seek some form of expression. Then the background becomes potentially charged in a new way in relation to character. It becomes an expression or reflection of character, worked up by an artist or artists for that purpose. And in the case of Bogart I know he is also the fictional detective named Philip Marlowe. I am unlikely to forget the fact entirely if I have followed his story up to this point. He is wary and cynical, sometimes unscrupulous, although he seems to uphold the prevailing moral order. Yet forces of degeneracy, perversion, and corruption continue to drag him deeper to a point of no return. His entrance to the house at the end of Laverne Terrace commits him, irrevocably, to the struggle with darkness. The shadows, the clutter, the sharp and twisting shapes together form a vision of what he dare not speak. They are his fears writ large, his confusion made tangible. They are condensed in the figure of the woman in the chair; she is an object of desire and thus of temptation. She is also one sign of the general enigma. She is mirrored by the hollow head of the Buddha to which the camera pans as Marlowe walks from her to it. A relay is established among people and things and this relay is a clue to the inner life of character. The setting is linked to character; it appears as one phase in the character's development, and therefore changes of setting signal changes of character. Philip Marlowe will return to this house several times. Only on the last occasion does he fire a gun. And in our fictional mode of looking we know what to think when he leaves the head of Buddha on the table all shot up (see figures I.1–I.6).

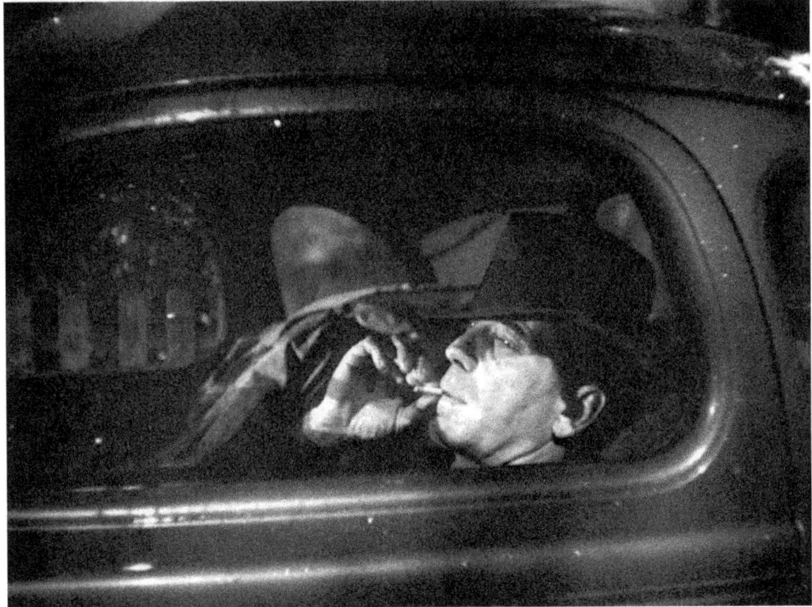

Figure I.1. *The Big Sleep*, dir. Howard Hawks, US, 1946. Digital frame grabs.

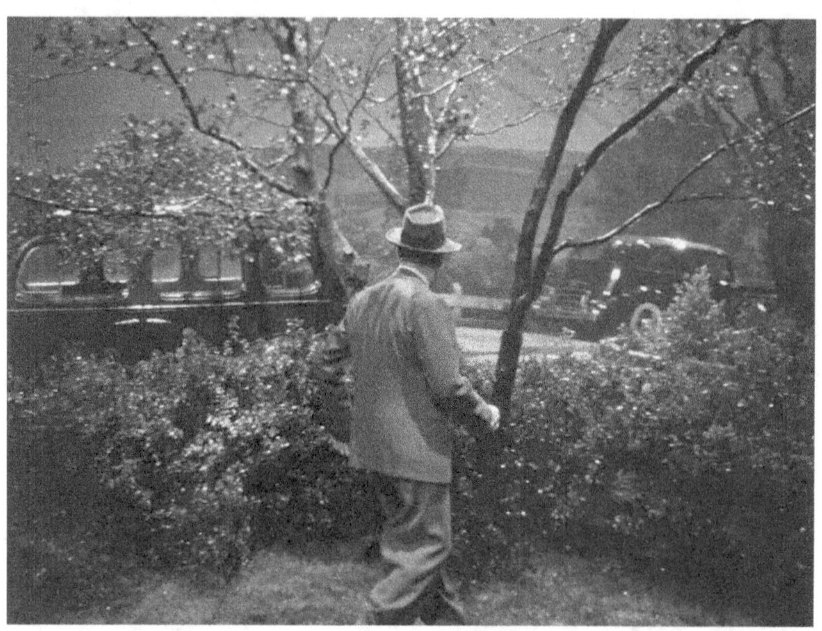

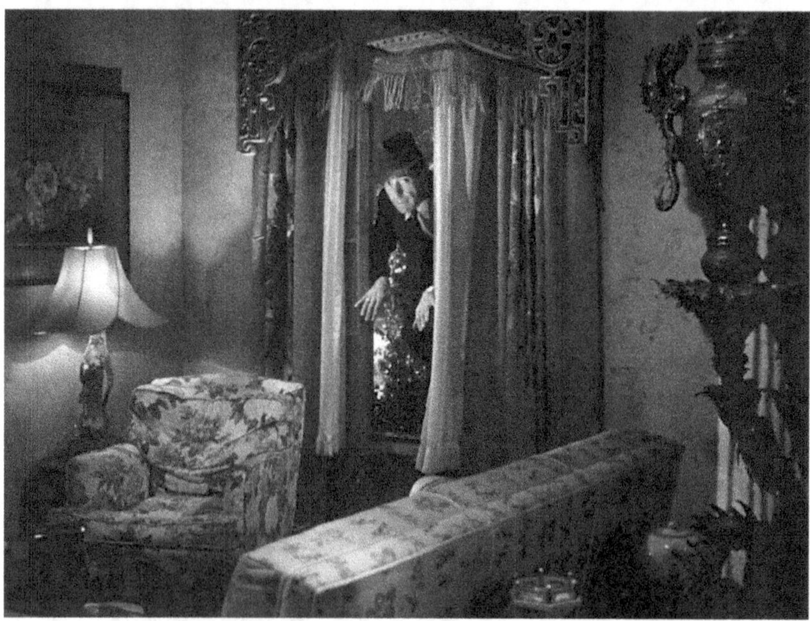

Figures I.2 and I.3. *The Big Sleep*, dir. Howard Hawks, US, 1946. Digital frame grabs.

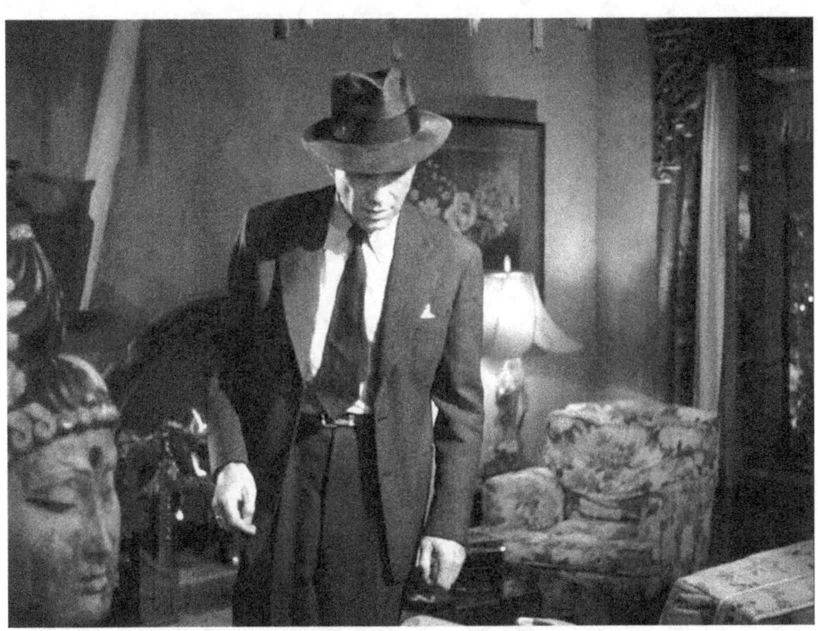

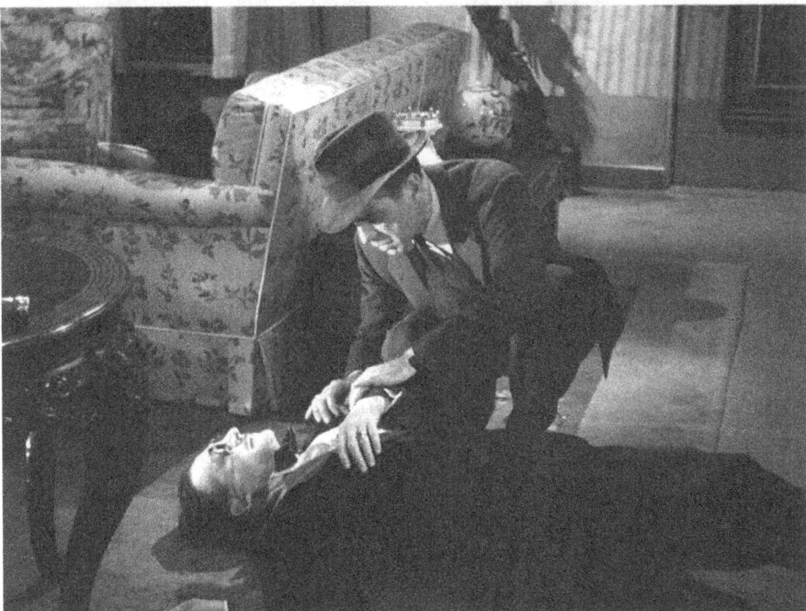

Figures I.4 and I.5. *The Big Sleep*, dir. Howard Hawks, US, 1946. Digital frame grabs.

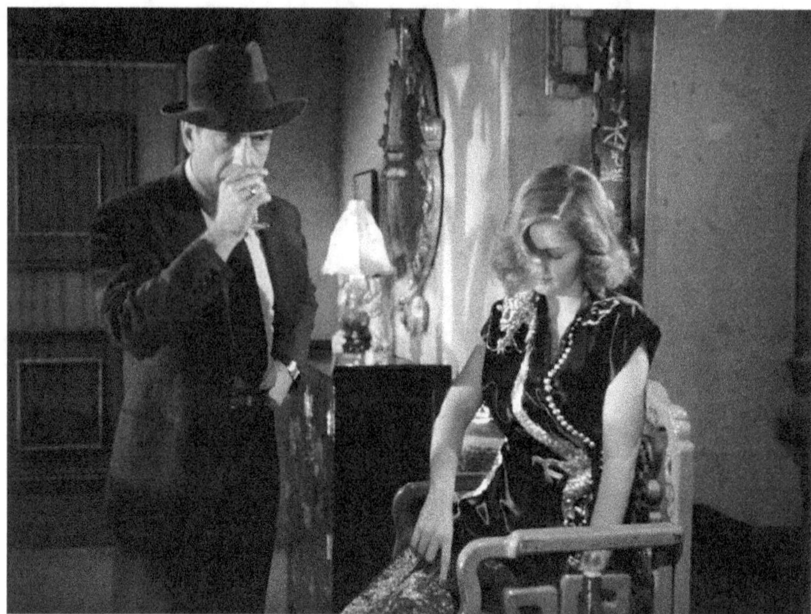

Figures I.6. *The Big Sleep*, dir. Howard Hawks, US, 1946. Digital frame grabs.

"Wonderful—ah, wonderful!" But somehow these words no longer fit the film before me.

Natural, pictorial, institutional, and fictional are the four modes of looking this study will treat. We normally use them all together, but we can, in analysis, privilege now one, now another mode of looking. Each is a specific optic, a way of looking at the human figure, a way of dealing with the people whose images we find on film. As methods or ways of seeing, they are obviously selective. Each commits us to the form of data that its guiding concept yields. And so, having chosen, we proceed in a way that resembles the way of science, for to think with criteria is a scientific project. One uses a concept or conceptual scheme to structure observation and yield a so-called truth. What counts as true will vary from one science to the next. Each has its operations, its standards of evidence, which may exclude without denying other concepts and standards. Each method has criteria that follow from its concept, whether natural, pictorial, institutional, or fictional. The concept, for its part, cannot claim objects that belong to it alone. Rather, it discloses an aspect of the same object that other concepts also cover while disclosing different aspects. Aristotle called this a distinction in the concept without a difference in the instance.[7] In our case the instance is the filmed human figure, which may serve all the concepts in succession or at once.

Natural, as we saw, means natural-historical, where the figure is the object of a natural history. Those who call themselves naturalists or natural historians will investigate that figure as a source of behaviors. And since every figure must have also its ground, the naturalist treats the figure as an organism in its environment. Environment includes objects and other nearby organisms as well as the terrain and the weather or climate.

The pictorial concept belongs at once to art history and visual psychology. Its figure is what is meant when artists speak of figure drawing, that is as a shape for pictorial manipulation. Its ground is the composition in which that shape is set, and this ground extends only to the borders of the frame. Knowledge of the figure then consists in the judgment of its role in composition and its contribution to aesthetic pleasure.

The institutional concept derives from social science, particularly anthropology. An institution is a form of social organization that endures long enough to be recognized and named: the family, the army, the school, political parties, and in our case the cinema. For movies are products of social organization—of a ground partly visible in the artifact itself. Their figures are units with defined social functions of which the most important is performance for the camera.

Fiction as a concept would seem to be self-evident. It names what is imaginary, or less factual than fact. Its ground is the self-enclosed fictional world it erects from the shards of reality that suit it. The critic of fiction sees figures as characters—as bundles of traits with goals and desires. And the setting or background in which the figure stands expresses those traits of character, those goals and desires; it expresses what is sometimes called a state of mind.

Definitions such as these are always too general. We shall not remain long in the realm of abstraction, for we want to see how the concepts will function in practice; how they frame and delimit and make knowledge from an object. To do so we require exemplars of all the concepts. Exemplars, for us, are thinkers with coherent and substantial oeuvres behind them. Coherence will derive from the force of a given concept, whose use we can study in depth and in detail. That is the strength of our approach by exemplars. But all writers inevitably have their eccentricities—habits and dispositions that limit the concept's range. The reader will do well to keep this in mind, for such is the price we pay for our fine-grained approach. Nonetheless I have tried to choose four exemplars that show the strengths and weaknesses of each favored concept. More important, they show how strength and weakness are intimately related; they illustrate contradictions, tensions in the concept, points at which it overlaps with the content of other concepts. They also illustrate the fact that the concept comes to life in a chain of operations performed on the filmic object. It makes a world of difference whether the human figure is viewed on a special projector for frame-by-frame viewing, or in sets of still images hung on the wall like paintings, or after conducting interviews with those involved in a film's production, or in a movie theater, larger than life. Yet these are the several methods of the writers I treat: Ray Birdwhistell, Victor Freeburg, Hortense Powdermaker, and V. F. Perkins. They exemplify, respectively, the natural, pictorial, institutional, and fictional as these are brought to bear on the filmed human figure. Their exemplary status is not incompatible with their eccentric or accidental features. With each standing in for other writers of a genus, they share the generic qualities bestowed by the guiding concept, but they are also individuals in a particular place and time. Their limitations should be obvious when we note that all were white, most of them were men, and all were employed at some point in higher education. Any concept of the figure is marked by exclusions, and when a writer selects it for use in a study, it is even more limited by her or his background. It is filtered by the writer's position in history. Hence this book, while not a history, treats its subjects historically. And since history involves diverse forms of practice—tools and techniques, accepted ways of doing—our book is necessarily a study in praxeology. We study the concept as realized in practice by historical agents who are typical and unique at once. The physical supports of their four ways of looking are definite ingredients in the concepts they produce. Diversity of tools should come as no surprise in the wild, early days of any young medium. But at the center of those efforts is the same raw material: the filmed human body, or rather, the human figure.

~

"It is an incontestable fact that in a motion picture no live human being is up there. But a human *something* is, and something unlike anything else we know."[8] What we choose to call this *something* is a matter of some importance. No amount of definition can negate what a word connotes. A word poorly chosen might lead us astray by provoking expectations that will then be disappointed. Our purpose in this study is to better understand how the human *something* on film becomes an object of knowledge. Knowledge, as I have said, implies use of criteria: rules of thumb by which the object is made to yield data. More simply it means that we ask certain questions that define in advance what will count as an answer. We want, therefore, a word for that *something* that accommodates many questions and yields many answers. Two words present themselves as obvious candidates, the figure on the one hand and the body on the other.

A figure is an object seen against a ground; it is something external, something over there. It has a definite contour that allows it to appear as separate from other figures, and especially from ourselves. If we refer to our own figures we already assume the stance of an outside observer seeing ourselves. The word is also used in the realm of mathematics and this gives to it a chilly, intellectual cast. Everyday language expresses this well. We figure out puzzles, riddles, and ciphers. We figure on having such and such an income when planning our outlay for the calendar year. We use figures of speech to point up an argument, or insert into our text some figures for illustration. A figure is something distant that we perceive and we perceive it because it is minimally distant. "I have tried to figure her out, I have thought about her as I might do about a problem in algebra."[9] Thus Dowell in Ford Madox Ford's *The Good Soldier*.

The body, on the other hand, seems somehow thicker: not merely because it has extension in space but because it suggests a thing with a certain depth and density. It has weight and resistance and it teems with inner life. Sometimes the inside bubbles over to the outside, in retching, belching, sneezing, and flatus, all of which are seen as causes of embarrassment. They embarrass because largely beyond our control.

Yet that loss of control has its own unique appeal. The body in all its thickness and wildness seems to escape the formalism that constrains the human figure—that turns human beings into human figures. For what can be figured can also be known: identified, tagged, reckoned with, dealt with. The body resists such knowledge; it resists in the absence of any conscious resistance, and so the contour by which any figure is bounded is shivered to pieces by eruptions of the body. The concept of *the body* comes to name whatever in us escapes form and power, as the sea escapes the net.

The Cinematic Body by Steven Shaviro offers illustration of this concept at work. Its politics are broadly antiestablishment, and the body is something that resists the establishment: capitalism, patriarchy, normative sexuality, or any discourse that polices the body's activity. This policing takes the form of representation with its ascription of identity to this or that body. Such tags of identity include, for example, the categories of gender, sexuality, and race. It is not enough for Shaviro to simply critique these categories as he finds them employed in the field of representation. "Too much has already been conceded," he writes, "when representation is accepted as the battlefield. It is necessary to go further."[10] The only way out from under the thumb of discourse is to embrace some other term that falls outside discourse. This term is the body, which is too much for discourse—"unruly," "transgressive," "asubjective," "immanent." It is profoundly mysterious. Hence rather than submit to the tyrannies of identity, one might instead submit to the powers of the body. Then, in the absence of structure, and of the tags of identity that limit its play, the body can do its work of liberation and negation. Then watching a film would be something other than cognitive activity based on visible and audible cues. Then it would be a form of surrender in which one is "violently, viscerally affected."[11] There would be no representation, and thus no repression, only the sights and sounds and the disturbances they generate.

So the cinematic body is the viewer's body. But it is not only the viewer's body. "There is," Shaviro writes, "a continuity between the physiological and affective responses of my own body and the appearances and disappearances, the mutations and perdurances, of the bodies and images on screen." Again, the film is a medium "for affirming, perpetuating, and multiplying" bodies. Each visible body "provokes and compels us." And thus we are forced "beyond a certain limit."[12] Such statements seem to follow more or less directly from use of the word *body* for viewer and image. If both bear the name, they must have something in common; perhaps there is even a degree of synchronicity. A writer would then be justified in sliding between them in the course of discussion of the cinematic body. Others have even called the camera a body, moving as it does through three-dimensional space; or called the film a body, which can manifest symptoms; or called the screen a skin, something all bodies have.[13] There would seem to be few limits to the word's application.

Certain is that language becomes a kind of shell game whose referent is lost in the textual shuffle—a game performed not with intent to deceive but to affirm a continuity across these phenomena. The body is that which "touches" and "wounds," and "abolishes the distances," so it cannot be thought or figured in any real sense.[14] It allows for a kind of free fall into immanence, where subject and object lose their distinctions. In other words the body is an anti-intellectual concept. Those writers who embrace its ambiguous reference do so to capture something real in their experience: the forgetting of ourselves in the course of a film's unfolding. But this forgetting is perhaps less frequent than they imagine. Again we might quote from *The Cinematic Body*, whose discussion of Jerry Lewis is characteristic and revealing.

"He experiences chaos in his own body; this chaos is then disseminated in waves around him."[15] The different iterations of the Lewis persona seem to tell a single story of a body beyond control. Whether costumed as a bellboy or hospital attendant, he brings about disorder by his excess of zeal. His body is so responsive to suggestions and commands that he executes them wildly, in no particular order. Breakdown soon manifests in spastic contortions, which in turn will produce the destruction of property. The breakdown spreads throughout the mise-en-scène; it reaches the other characters and eventually hits the audience. Shaviro calls it "contagion," a transmissible fever that makes the viewer share in the joy of abandon.[16] There is no conscious assent; the image "provokes and compels" and the body accedes before the mind has time to stop it. The task of the writer is to convey this excitement of a body-to-body linkage—convey it in prose that reflects the loss of self and therefore of any intellectual distinctions. That is why it is so remarkable that distinctions should creep back in. For the manifest irrationalism of the description is tempered by criteria, that is to say thinking, and in a single datum like the body of Jerry Lewis one finds levels and degrees, aspects and sides. There is, for one, the biological organism "in its inertia and its dense plasticity." As the organism is progressively shaken by impulse, it produces for the viewer some "strange, ungainly shapes."[17] And this particular viewer who committed his thoughts to writing knew Lewis already as a star with a life offscreen, known for his "philanthropic endeavor and appeals to public sympathy."[18] But, in his films, he puts this energy to other uses; he plays fictional characters with clear-cut desires, like the bellboy whose driving goal "is to become an obedient employee."[19] Thus the writer finds four different aspects of the object: natural, pictorial, institutional, and fictional. He makes the object yield different answers to his questions. He makes from its body a fourfold human figure as a gem cutter works up a rough piece of stone. Let us work the stone further in the chapters to follow. We will generally opt to call it the filmed human figure without being too pedantic about this distinction.

~

Elias Canetti once wrote of the process of composing his novel *Auto-da-Fé* (1935): "I tried to help myself by forming strands, a few individual features, which I tied to human beings; this brought the beginning of perspicuity into the mass of experiences."[20] He gave to them each a guiding obsession as well as a language in which to express it. So the scholar thinks only of his thousands of books; his maid, of the money she can make from his books; and Fischerle, of chess. Despite their narrow limits, they have "daring, surprising thoughts."[21] Their forms of expression are "precious and unique." We learn something important when we follow them each in detail. Hidden aspects of experience, hidden because alloyed, come out with the clarity of chemical elements. The will to know, or acquire, or compete and strike down are given form within the shapes that these characters describe. Yet even their author did not want their borders to be so clear and hard that interaction was foreclosed. He imagined them all together in a pavilion for madmen; he hoped that in the end "they would talk to one another." Our concepts are also like this. Hence we put in place a rule that might foster their talking. We state it here again: the overlap of concepts. And so our stone is somewhat worn around the edges of its facets.

1

Natural (Ray L. Birdwhistell)

The proper study of man is man, said the poet, but there have been tacit limits to what that study consists of. One does not look too closely at the behavior of human beings. Those who do, for private or professional reasons, seem to remove themselves from the common human stream. They reduce their fellow people to the level of insects. They cannot help but do so when, like Monsieur Lecoq, they want to infer the secrets of those they suspect. At one point Lecoq goes so far as to make a hole in the roof of a prisoner's cell. This prisoner has a secret: he is not who he says he is; that much is obvious but difficult to prove. Only the patterns of his behavior will point a detective in the right direction. There Lecoq will sit, day after day, moving from the spot only when nature calls. He lies on his stomach with an eye pressed against the very small hole he has bored in the wood. We can hear the note of mania despite the reasonable assumptions that justify his plan for continuous observation. "I want to learn this prisoner's secret; and I will do so," he says. "I shall be present if ever his will fails him, if, believing himself alone, he lets his mark fall, or forgets his part for an instant, if an indiscreet word escapes him in his sleep, if his despair elicits a groan, a gesture, or a look—I shall be there to take note of it." We can also hear the note of anger mixed with the sarcasm of his superior, Inspector Gevrol. "Do you know what you will look like, with your eye glued to that hole?" he asks. "Ah, well! you will look just like one of those silly naturalists who put all sorts of little insects under a magnifying glass, and spend their lives in watching them." "You couldn't have found a better comparison," Lecoq replies. "What they can do with an insect, I will do with a man."[1] Our sense of embarrassment even today, when we see the results of such behavioral study, probably arises when we imagine for ourselves what we would reveal to such an observer. Few want to be the object of a natural history.

"Natural history," says a book on the subject, is "the study of life at the level of the individual—of what plants and animals do."[2] They do certain things in relation to each other and to an environment for which they are adapted. An environment is full of resources that can be exploited. Among these resources are other living things. The animal organism finds others like itself with whom it can communicate for cooperative ends. The patterns of communication are a part of its behavior as it moves through the phases of life to its death. Each of those phases is a part of its natural history, and each contains behavior that is largely repetitive. Outside observers, natural historians, can record that behavior for reference and study. They seek what is typical in the particular; they record the behavior of samples or specimens. And they aim to record this in an unobtrusive way so that the behavior occurs as if observers were not there. For they want to know what organisms really do together, and in what contexts they do it, typically and spontaneously—in a word, naturally. The stance thus assumed is called objectivity.

There is no particular reason one cannot be objective with humans as well as plants and nonhuman animals, and the camera has often been used as an aid to objective recording of human behavior. Even before cinema made it easy to reproduce the flow of behavior as seen with our eyes, there are notable attempts to do so with the older technology, in particular with rapid, serial still photography. Eadweard Muybridge's work is the most famous of these attempts. As early as 1878 he used a row of cameras to record the linear movement of a horse in its paces. He refined the technique in subsequent years, and he managed to make the intervals so short that we now make little movies from the stills that survive. Not only animal but also human behavior came within his purview as a research photographer, and among the last products of his professional life was a book with the title *The Human Figure in Motion* (1901). Thus Muybridge would seem to claim a certain precedence in any discussion of the natural human figure. But Muybridge was not really a natural historian. True, his aim was to capture the typical behaviors of children and adults, women and men. He showed them walking, running, leaping, using tools, and he showed them as specimens of the larger human family. Yet all of them were photographed in lab-like conditions. Each subject performed his or her behavior sequence at the photographer's prompting and was asked to do it naked. And each was removed from any normal surroundings to be framed against a coordinate grid in the background. In all but several instances they were shot in isolation from the other men and women with whom they might commune. Hence what Muybridge recorded was behavior in a vacuum, lasting some seconds, unrelated to anything or anyone else. A proper natural history would have to be done with spontaneous behavior in a typical environment, in a context allowing for social interaction. Muybridge did, however, affirm in his photography that the figure in motion should be seen from head to toe. This was an important precedent.

~

When the anthropologist Ray L. Birdwhistell began to use film for the serious study of human behavior, the all-inclusive full shot became his basic unit. He needed the human figure as seen from head to toe, in the presence of other figures as seen from head to toe—needed it for complicated theoretical reasons that, nonetheless, have the simplicity of parable. "John does not communicate to Mary, and Mary does not communicate to John," he wrote. "Mary and John engage in communication."[3] They do so with all their senses, at every moment of their encounter, and insofar as they are organisms they cannot help but do this. For an organism lives in dynamic exchange with the several components of its environment, from earliest gestation to its final decay and death. This is why Birdwhistell studied kinesics, his word for what we usually call body motion, but it is also why he spoke of context analysis, where "a person is a moment in this order of theorizing."[4] A close-up of someone, whatever the gain in detail, is just a fragment of a fragment of a fragment of context. Thus two or more figures fill Birdwhistell's frame.

He earned his PhD in anthropology from the University of Chicago in 1951. A vague urge to be useful brought him to the U.S.

Foreign Service Institute the following year.[5] There he completed a prospectus for future work, the *Introduction to Kinesics*, which brought him some fame beyond his profession. His friend Al Capp created the character "Professor Fleasong" for three Sunday installments of the cartoon *Li'l Abner*.[6] Walt Disney, supposedly, offered Birdwhistell employment. True or not, he pursued a conventional academic career. He taught at the University of Louisville, then the University of Buffalo, and finally the University of Pennsylvania. There was, however, a rather long period where he worked in a clinic as a senior research scientist. There was a good deal of funding for health-related work that made this arrangement both feasible and attractive. Thus while early research in the field of kinesics used naturalistic street scenes, it increasingly relied on filmed psychotherapy. Birdwhistell, a compelling speaker with a certain gift for mime, often appeared on TV or radio in this period. Naturally, he talked about kinesics, which he pronounced with a hard *i* and a long *e*. It is doubtful that anyone understood the details but all were excited by the promise of kinesics. Men, especially, seemed to think it would help to further the art of the sexual pickup.[7]

Technical details of kinesics are unimportant for our purposes; a brief outline is enough to give a sense of its procedures. Its units of analysis are all modeled on linguistics, particularly linguistics of the structural variety. The *kine* is the smallest perceptible unit of difference and the *kineme*, a unit that people recognize as meaningful. Just as the "p" in *pin* and the "p" in *spin* are technically different but both grouped in the phoneme /p/, there are dozens of physical positions of an eyebrow but perhaps only three that we really perceive as different. We can stare, squint, or keep our eyebrows at rest. These, then, are the kinemes of kinesics. Two or more kinemes used simultaneously make a word-like unit known as a *kinemorph*, and a succession of such units makes a kinemorphic construction. There are also kinesic markers of stress, as well as kinesic modifiers, such as a posture one sustains. All of this is formalized in a complex notation that Birdwhistell said would take five years to master.[8] But he intended it only as a means to an end, the study of body motion as an aspect of culture (see figure 1.1).

It was Birdwhistell's fieldwork as a graduate student that confirmed the importance for him of kinesics. In Kentucky he was struck

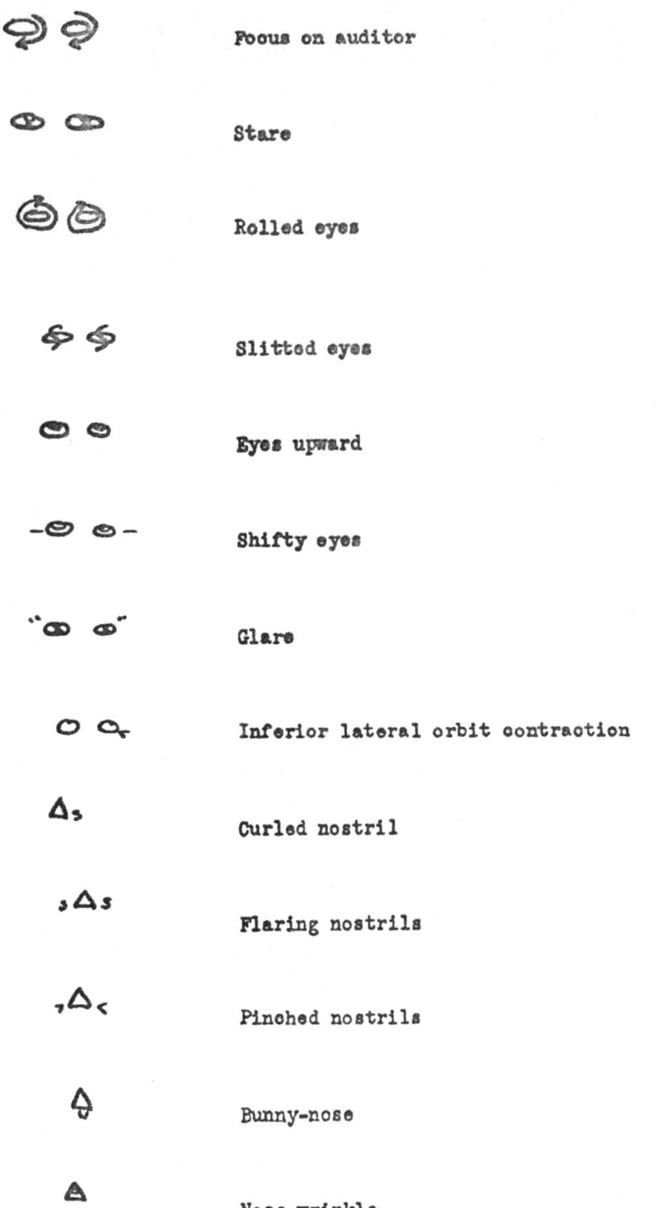

Figure 1.1. Kinegraphs of the face area. From Ray L. Birdwhistell, *Introduction to Kinesics* (1952).

by the ways that different districts expressed the signs of illness. Of particular importance were the months that he spent among the Ktunaxa in British Columbia. They impressed him with their ability to easily distinguish between themselves and whites when seen at great distances. The sign of the difference was the way each group walked. That is something one learns from earliest childhood; it is part of the training for life in this culture. It must be absorbed by the sensitive organism from the example of others in its environment. Hence a baby must do more than grow as fast as possible. He must also, says Birdwhistell, "convince the world to accept him and not to kill him or let him die."[9] To do so he learns the culture down to the smallest details, even if no one tutors him in gait style explicitly. Society tends toward unity because it tends toward survival, and surely kinesics has a part in all this.

This much Birdwhistell learned from his graduate training in social anthropology. His fascination with the human figure, however, seems to begin much earlier—perhaps as early as he started to go to the movies. In the late 1930s he worked as an usher in a small movie theater in Oxford, Ohio, where he watched the same two features "over and over."[10] Though conventional films are what he came to reject, it is interesting to consider the continuity of experience. As late as 1955 he is still recommending the two-reeler *Sports Day* (1945) as an object of study. Of course, it must be viewed repetitively before one can see the patterns of behavior that it contains. This could take as many as ten to fifteen viewings and even then there may be things that one is quite blind to. None of Birdwhistell's students saw, for example, "the amount of body contact between the girl and the men," or rather they saw without really perceiving.[11]

Birdwhistell does not elaborate, but we can turn to the film itself.[12] A boy is accused at school of animal cruelty and is punished with detention on the annual sports day. The classmates who accuse him are really responsible. They want him out of the picture so he cannot compete against them. His sister undertakes to clear him of blame by appealing to the headmaster whose dog had been injured. Played by Jean Simmons at the age of fifteen, the role has what Birdwhistell calls a seductive quality. Seduction as a means to righting moral wrongs is hardly the message this film would convey. Yet there is no denying this aspect of her performance as soon as one knows to look for the behavior. She comes to the gate of the headmaster's garden. Grasping a bar, she fixes her hair quickly and opens the gate. She walks through the garden in very low light, looking here and there for the master of the house. He addresses her from the shadows of the veranda. She approaches apologetically. Urging her to sit, he touches her upper arms without actually grabbing or using much pressure. Instinctively she smiles and brings her left hand up to touch his right forearm with her extended fingers. She continues to smile and gaze into his eyes as she lowers herself into a chair. His right hand withdraws but his left hand remains on her shoulder as long as possible, until she is seated. This physical interaction lasts roughly five seconds. "Well, I'm Tom Hill's sister," she tells him. "Then Tom is a very lucky fellow," he replies. Soon they leave arm in arm to relieve her brother from detention. Later, watching the boy compete, she sits in a chair and the headmaster stands behind her. His hand is on her shoulder and she grasps it in excitement. And when the brother wins, she stands up and throws her long, bare arms around the blushing headmaster. Even the male teacher standing beside them grazes and pats the girl when he has opportunity. Older men touch her more often than we expect them or, at any rate, more than we care to see. It may not be something the actors care to see either and might even prove embarrassing if brought to their attention (see figures 1.2 and 1.3).

Thus even the studio film, for all its unreality, can yield quite a lot of natural-history data. Such a film, however, has several limitations if one believes that whole figures must be shown for long periods. Many small decisions have already been made regarding how much of the figures we see. People are generally cut off at the chest or waist, sometimes at the knees, almost never at the feet so that they appear in full. Shots are rarely more than five or six seconds, and they frequently isolate one figure from the others. Most of the behavior is hidden, screened off; what is left has been fitted into a new conception. "Any time you fool with the verities of a culture, you get in trouble," said Birdwhistell.[13] There was no question in his mind that film was essential. The only question was the type of film he should try to obtain. It was, in the end, the ethnographic films that proved most decisive as an influence on Birdwhistell, for the best of these films were shot in long stretches and often in long

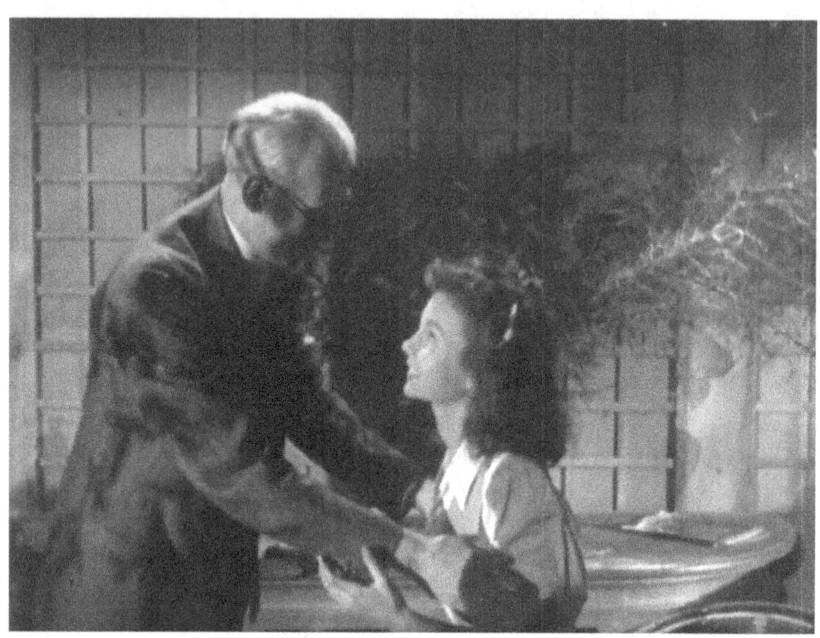

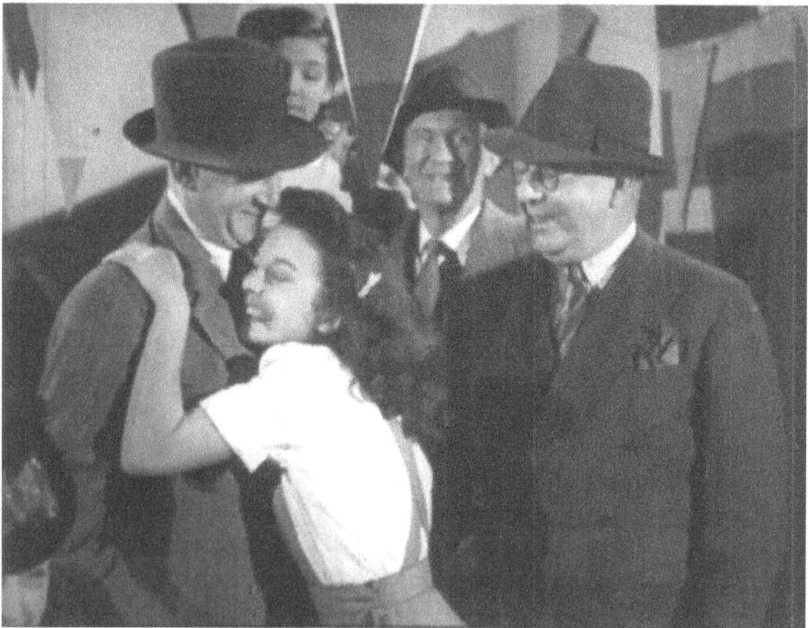

Figures 1.2 and 1.3. *Sports Day*, also known as *Colonel's Cup*, dir. Francis Searle, UK, 1945. Digital frame grabs.

shot, unlike conventional movies.[14] Such a style had not been seen much since the earliest silent films that imitated theater.[15] But even ethnographic films made too many prejudgments in terms of what they choose to frame and record, and it turned out that Birdwhistell would have to make the films himself to furnish material for rigorous study.

A film of social interaction for behavioral research had to preserve its object in a particular way. It had to be a record of one or more people seen in full figure and acting spontaneously. The camera, for its part, was to be anything but spontaneous. Rules were put in place to eliminate spontaneity. The cinematographer was strictly a camera technician who set up the lights and turned the camera on. When the subject to be filmed was two people in dialogue, the camera showed them from head to toe for the entire length of filming. The same went for three, four people or more. All would be compassed until the frame was fit to burst. A second camera could shoot simultaneously if, for some reason, close-ups were needed. Naturally such a setup favored immobility: people around a table, in a pub, or on a couch. Where the entertainment film would begin to cut among them, the scientific camera was cold and phlegmatic. It remained fixed and neutral in the interest of objectivity. To zoom in for a close-up, to pan or cut between close-ups, is to give a judgment on the nature of the thing recorded. For the close-up says implicitly, This item is important. And the reverse-shot says implicitly, This relation is important. Such devices, in a way, mimic common sense, or rather common sense derives from such devices. But common sense is stupid. More charitably, it is deluded. It sees what it wants to see in accord with some ideal.

"In the novel, and even more clearly, in the drama, we find individuals who speak politely in turn," writes Birdwhistell. We see John speak to Mary and Mary to John, in regular alternation, with words that come from their heads. "One day in the average home or office reveals how poetic is such a conception."[16] Of course it is convenient to see just a head when common sense assigns it such outsize importance; then to see the other head to whom it has spoken. But then one will never know if the movement of Mary's foot has anything to do with John's last response, or if the presence of someone else guided both of their behavior. Thus the research film must offer a continuous record of social interaction in the most styleless style of all so that no detail, however trivial, is denied its rightful place. The very concept of triviality is abolished by such a film.

Of the films now extant and cosigned by Birdwhistell, *The Hillcrest Family* (1968) most fully satisfies those criteria. The bulk of it consists of four half-hour reels that record a course of therapy with a family of six. Each reel, however, is done with a different therapist so that viewers can compare four therapy styles. The parents are in therapy because of the strain of four children from three different marriages including their own. In particular, the oldest, an eleven-year-old boy has a penchant for stealing and general misbehavior. His biological father and his fairly new stepmother are often at odds with regard to his discipline. The family plus the therapist make for a scene of seven, all of them in one shot from their heads to their toes.

The film is from the years that Birdwhistell held his research position at a clinic in Philadelphia. The Eastern Pennsylvania Psychiatric Institute produced many films under his general direction. He designed and had built a soundstage of sorts for natural-history filming of very high quality. The irony was not lost on him but he tried to ensure that it resembled a doctor's office as much as was possible. The only real difference was the presence of the camera and a certain artificial quality in the arrangement of the chairs. The family and their doctor are seated in a crescent for maximum visibility of faces and hands. Their angles range from frontal to three-quarter views, and at the same time there are mirrors on the wall behind them; hence their hither sides are not lost to the camera. The camera itself is placed about twenty-five feet away on a tripod or table, in full view of everyone. It was hoped that the subjects would learn to ignore it. The technicians were no distraction because they could leave after the camera began to shoot. A 1,200-foot magazine of 16mm film could last without a reel change for up to thirty minutes; a wide-angle lens ensured everything was captured. Hence the record was perfect, isomorphic with its object, and hundreds of therapies were filmed in this fashion. People stay seated in the course of therapy, anyway. The only exceptions are very young children, especially the baby on the floor in this film. But even the children's movements in and out of frame are useful in provoking the husband's and wife's responses. Their different reactions to their children's behavior is precisely what the sessions of the film are most concerned with. What the image uniquely allows us to see are the visible components of one's total response. The movement of the figures affirms or negates their talk, or else it expresses what they can't or dare not say. And the cooccurring movements of two or more figures is an ongoing commentary on their relation.

Though Birdwhistell published nothing on *The Hillcrest Family*, some of his students did in the form of a didactic film. They looked at the reel of Dr. Don Jackson with "a natural-history method developed by Birdwhistell."[17] The lecturers stand in front of a chart that plots the course of movements for all three adults. They replay the footage at slower speed than normal, often masking off portions of the frame for convenience. Though the hosts are not especially dynamic speakers, they help us see patterns in the behavior. For instance, every time that Jackson changes the subject from the boy's disobedience to the ways his parents deal with it, the wife leans away from her husband beside her. Further, she crosses her arms in a defensive maneuver. And every time Jackson does make this gambit, he hunches over, clasps his hands, then resumes his normal posture. "With this method we're concerned not with the interpretation of meaning on a clinical level," say the hosts. They avoid any reference to what is not there in the frame. When the eleven-year-old boy steps away for a moment and returns with a small rocking chair that he has found, he places it in front of him to rock with his feet. "We might interpret the action with the empty chair as a signal involving the missing mother" but we would be in error, even if the doctor mentioned her. Our task is not to interpret at all. We must treat the chair merely as an object he plays with and since he plays with it only once, it is less important than others.

Such is Birdwhistell's lesson for these of his students. Their attention is not allowed to seize on some particular, then to go on and find meaning behind it. Instead they are forced to stay at the surface and disperse their attention across the whole frame. Strange things start to happen to the filmed human figure. It too is dispersed across the whole frame. It divides into pieces that may be related to any other piece of figure that is framed along with it. A woman crosses her arms and this crossing says something about the system she is part of. The cross has meaning only in relation to other units, which may or may not belong to her figure. They may well belong to the figures of those around her, for instance to her husband's figure when he leans away. No movement is treated as a thing in itself, nor does it express the inner feelings of the mover; rather it is seen in the context of all the movements performed by the ensemble of natural figures. Its meaning is nothing more than its placement in a sequence. It finds surprising echoes in the environment and is bound to other movements by new threads of identity. The natural historians who make these connections are tying the pieces of figures together. They connect part to part, part to whole, whole to part, until the image becomes a tapestry of human communication. Someone leans forward, another's arms are crossed, and these become part of one meaningful cluster. Thus patterns emerge from a manifold of interaction that initially seems to have no structure at all.

And that is hard work for the natural historian. It requires what Birdwhistell liked to call discipline. The technique that he developed and described in publications is a total technique for film production and analysis.[18] The analysis is geared toward a certain kind of film and the film is produced with the analysis in mind. The film, as we saw, is to be an inclusive record of a social interaction in its actual duration. It has figures as seen from their heads to their toes and it lets the camera run as long as technically possible. The film is then submitted to a standard procedure. First it is reprinted with a numerical overlay so that each frame is numbered from 0 to *n*. One might see, for example, that an arm cross begins on frame 028800 and that it ends ten frames later. The frame begins to function as a clock for its own contents, and it allows for citation and recheck by others. One can tell if a film was prepared for analysis simply by the presence of these overlaid numbers. The numbers have only a rough relation, though, to a first phase of viewing that is sometimes called "soaking." The word suggests immersion, or acclimation to another temperature. It consists of watching films perhaps a dozen or fifty times under normal conditions, at the standard rate of playback. One then becomes attuned to the structure of interaction. What first seems like nothing but two people talking breaks down into chunks with a certain integrity, and from an unshaped mass of film one emerges with "scenes." One emerges, that is, with an impression of order and even of narrative in the interaction. Turning points, climaxes, or the establishment of intimacy are signaled by movements and large shifts in posture. After the soaking phase comes analysis proper, either of the whole film or of specific scenes. There are various degrees of smallness one can use, "maybe eighth-seconds for a microanalysis and one- or three-second intervals for a more gross analysis."[19] Limb by limb, kineme by kineme, the eye performs a kind of scansion of the retarded film. It looks at movements in one figure, then at another, and within each one it looks at the several regions separately: the head, the face, the trunk, the arms, the hands, the legs, the feet, the neck. Those kinesic units that are sifted or sculptured out are plotted simultaneously on scrolls of graph paper. A ruled metal board with variegated magnets might also suffice if the units are well-known. Patterns can now be seen at a glance and possible groupings circled for later comparison.

All of this relies on special projectors, usually known as analyst or time-and-motion projectors. Clear images, rich in detail, easily replayed are absolute necessities in microkinesic work. A standard film projector cannot serve this purpose; the heat of its lamp burns a hole in the frame when paused. Flatbed editors are better but will often cause eyestrain from the small and poorly focused pictures they provide. Analyst projectors are especially designed for time-and-motion study in scientific work. The automatic models allow for film playback at twenty-four frames per second and at many speeds below this—all the way down to one frame per second. They can also advance the film by one single frame, hold it there indefinitely, then advance the film another frame when the analyst chooses. There is no strobing or flicker and it does not burn the filmstrip, although it is not unusual to wear out many prints. That is because one is rewatching segments dozens, hundreds, maybe thousands of times. Manual or hand-cranked models are marred by some flicker but have their advantages for microscopic work, like the ability to watch three or four frames repeatedly and at something approaching the normal speed of playback. Hence the figures move like people instead of toy soldiers, which is often how they look when run through automatics. The student of behavior has options to choose from.

The student has options proportionate to his budget, which in Birdwhistell's case is generous indeed. He has many thousands of dollars to dispose of at the height of his fame in the mid-1960s. His days are passed in and out of the lab in the practiced observation of human behavior. With a record in hand, stored in a canister, he subjects that behavior to segmentation and description. He has gadgets all around him that enable him to do so. He may even have one in the privacy of his office. The analyst projector lets him pause, rewind, pause, and resume until units are found and stream becomes structure. So he identifies patterns and notes them on a graph. Then he compares them to other parts of the film, or to similar situations in yet other films. Some data are obvious and go without saying; some are so shocking that few eyes will see them. He sees them, though, because he is disciplined. Repetition wears away the constraints of his morality. Perhaps it takes thirty sessions before he can see that a little boy on film is touching his penis. Still, he sees it and notes it. He marks it on the graph among other movements in his pursuit of totality, the exhaustion of the filmstrip. He can watch a film again and again and continue to enrich his understanding of its contents. How could he not? A newly observed datum, one-eighth of a second, might change the whole picture he now has before him.

Many things can happen in one-eighth of a second. Time itself is dense when two people meet. It is richer in incident than one can possibly dream of and full of hidden dangers when the meeting goes awry. The following is one such instance of microscopic danger. It is a film by Gregory Bateson from the mid-1950s, made as part of a study of family dynamics. It shows a suburban housewife with her children at home. There are smiles, there is role-play; afternoon light floods the dinette. One girl, an infant, receives a warm bath. The bath itself lasts just over four minutes. What precedes it, says Birdwhistell, is truly disturbing. We must look very closely in order to see why. And we must, of course, be willing to see, for the content may affront our most tender feelings. It consists of the mother's removing the young girl's diaper, which is made out of cloth and fastened with a pin. The action breaks down into many smaller actions, not all of them in harmony, when we reduce the scale of viewing to eighth-of-a-second intervals.

The task is accomplished in forty-three frames, a little less than two seconds of movie time. Frames 0 to 9 show the mother's hand as it both removes the diaper and keeps the girl's hand from the pin. That is, while the mother with her fingers is undoing the pin, she uses the wrist of the very same hand to push the girl's away from that which might harm it. The girl, accordingly, lifts her arm up and grabs a nearby curtain at a level with her head. Frames 10 to 21 show a different kinesic signal as the mother, still fumbling, now uses the wrist to depress the girl's abdomen. This makes the girl let go of the curtain and bring her hand down in the direction of the pressure.

Frame 28 is something else again. The mother, it seems, "sends both messages at once, seemingly emphasizing one of the messages somewhat more strongly than the other." She sends the message *up* as well as the message *down*. By frame 42, "the baby's hand is moving again."[20] But the sign of confusion is forever upon her. Diapers are changed six or more times a day, every single day of a child's first few years of life, and one can assume that this or that changing is more or less like all the others and perhaps like other actions. Each is an occasion for the mix-up of signals. The signals strike the girl without resolution and leave disfiguring marks on her pattern of behavior. When babies become toddlers "they are very old indeed," having lived through tens of millions of intervals like this one.[21]

Such bad communication or mix-up of signals mortifies the child who cannot escape it. For the child can never raise and lower her arm at once, never satisfy both conditions, and yet she would do anything to please the one who mothers. She wants to be loved and cared for; she does not want to die. She must, then, learn to smile and nod. Gradually she learns to ignore her true feelings. The result is persistent logical confusion and eventually schizophrenia, which is a communication illness. That is what we are seeing, writes Birdwhistell: the genesis of illness in eighth-of-a-second intervals. This mother was filmed because her own behavior pattern had shown some resemblance to schizophrenic detachment. Her older son already shows problems in living while the younger son looks healthy, at least "at first glance." It is too soon to tell how the girl will turn out but the prognosis is grim on the basis of the film. At least, it seems unpromising on the basis of these forty-three frames.

The natural-history figure is a "compositional" figure.[22] It is seen as composed of all the encounters that it has had and is currently having. But it is also compositional in a second sense, for it contributes its movements to a greater whole. It is part of a structure that transcends and enfolds it; it is only one element in a composition. Thus the separate status of organism and environment starts to become confused within this mode of looking. At first it seems that other organisms are an aspect of the environment in relation to the organism we apprehend as figure. Now they join up with the single, central organism to form a superorganism of many limbs and heads.

Here a bit of history is useful for context. The 1940s saw the birth of interpersonal psychiatry. It was a school that gave emphasis to the context of psychosis, especially to factors that maintain the psychotic process. It focused just as much on the present as on the past; it was thus a departure from psychoanalysis. The illness was freed from the confines of one psyche and became an ill relation among several people. Such themes were developed further in the 1950s with the rise of family therapy in the US. What people say and do to each other makes them ill, beginning in earliest childhood, in the bosom of the family—so it was argued. Parents and children communicate often, sometimes continuously for extended periods. In doing this, they repeat; they begin to establish patterns. The children bring these patterns with them to adulthood. Thus the family is the patient for the family therapist. The family is the organism that is treated and restored to health by the gambits and interventions of the observant therapist. It is made up of organs called parents and children, husband and wife, who give and get signals as organs secrete chemicals. But to really understand this, one must see how a family lives. One goes to its home with a notepad or camera, preferably a camera so that the data can be seen by others. This is all that Bateson really had in mind when he filmed children's baths and other domestic incidents. He was one of the pioneers of family therapy research although he was not himself a therapist and never would be.[23] He was trained as an anthropologist, much like the younger Birdwhistell. Both were dazzled by the prospect of a social science unified by concepts of interaction, communication, systems. It was hardly surprising that both found themselves working on a project at Stanford with psychiatrists and linguists also. To these Bateson gave his family film footage.

One film in particular captured the group's attention. It shows a woman on a couch, talking to Bateson, with her four-year-old son intermittently visible. They are in the woman's house; it is a house visit. It has something of the character of an informal interview. Mundane though it seems, it gave a foundation for a study of some importance: the way human beings become what they are. Those who saw the film would ultimately spend several years on its study and recruit yet more observers. They handled different aspects according to their training but they agreed that there was order at all points in interaction. Their motto was simply that "nothing never happens," that anything is a possible signal; therefore everything is relevant until proven otherwise.[24] They started to attack the film with this precept to guide them. That was in 1956, and the project was known as *The Natural History of an Interview*.[25]

The film itself was coded *GB-SU-005*. Most today know it as simply "the Doris film."[26] It is said that "Doris" reached out to Bateson after seeing him lecture in northern California; she asked to participate in his research on families. She had a child of four named "Billy" with some behavioral problems and was herself quite unhappy in her married, adult life. No doubt she was chafing under the limits of her role as an intelligent housewife with few outlets for expression. "I'd like to throw rocks through the window," she says elsewhere, and "tear the walls down."[27] But these walls are reaffirmed by the borders of the frame. And the frame of the film delimits the scope of her problems. Those who worked in family therapy saw illness as a social product but their purview generally ended with the four walls of a house. What falls outside the frame may as well not exist anyway for the purposes of natural-history description.

The Doris film is roughly ten minutes long, the length of three 100-foot 16mm rolls. The filming is continuous except for the gaps where the camera was reloaded with a new roll of film. Bateson and his cameraman visited Doris in the late afternoon after phoning just before. "She had just returned from a session with the therapist, had picked Billy up from the house of a neighbor, and was exhibiting the expectable responses of a housewife unprepared to receive her visitors."[28] In the film she plies Bateson with her own homemade beer as they settle on the couch for an informal talk. Much of it concerns her trouble with the child while the child is in earshot, running around with toys. The first roll begins with a full shot of Doris and Bateson on the sofa and Billy on the floor. A microphone juts into the frame at one corner. Both adults are smoking and Doris holds her mug of beer, although she never seems to drink any in these ten minutes. She begins to recount her problems with nursing when the child was still an infant a few years ago. "Every time he cried I would feel guilty because I would think, well he's just going to cry and what else to do and [my husband] would be hovering . . ." She resented the doctor's order for regular, frequent feedings, which made her "tired and nervous," as she tells Bateson. At this point the boy springs up with a toy he is fondling. He exits the frame, reenters soon after. Then he crosses the room and disappears offscreen left.

The camera zooms in to isolate Doris in a medium close-up, panning slightly as she reclines. Her husband, she continues, kept saying the boy was hungry; the doctor would say he was eating too much; "and this made a real nice situation all the way around." Now the camera zooms out as Billy returns with a cushion or pillow he hands to his mother. She places it behind her, unsure of the child's intention. The boy departs and the zoom is adjusted to reinclude Bateson, who sips his beer politely. He has largely been silent. For Doris is giddy and talks very quickly. It would be difficult for anyone to get a word in. The camera pans with Billy as he handles a toy airplane, which he also gives Doris, and continues to pan as he paces the room. Three minutes have elapsed when the roll of film ends; the second and third rolls are much like the first.

Birdwhistell found the film of much interest, though he lamented the zooms and panning the photographer indulged in. His interest did not stop at forty-three frames: nothing less than all ten minutes of the Doris film would do. He intended to write the history of these figures in their environment, an environment consisting partly of each other's sounds and movements. Maybe not every sound and movement was relevant to interaction but to decide this in advance would be a poor method. The film should be approached like an unknown universe for study. Even the smallest, poorest units might make some contribution. As many of them as possible would have to be transcribed in a consistent orthography, both linguistic and kinesic. In the final study published in 1971, every third frame is serially accounted for. Hence the transcription runs over four hundred pages. And it was still incomplete in Birdwhistell's view. "Tens of thousands of scientist hours have been applied to the study of this conversation," he said. "I doubt seriously that more than fifty percent of the significant data has been located and abstracted."[29] His sheets of transcription are utterly opaque but have a strange beauty, like musical staffs (see figures 1.4 and 1.5).

For one who can read them, or have them explained, they provide a common basis for inferences in prose. Each author of *The Natural History of an Interview* drew his own conclusions about the Doris film. All agree, however, that she seems uninvolved with the people around her. Her flurries of talk and movement give way on inspection to this wall against which the child knocks for entry. But beneath the missed connections is a thorough involvement in the process of

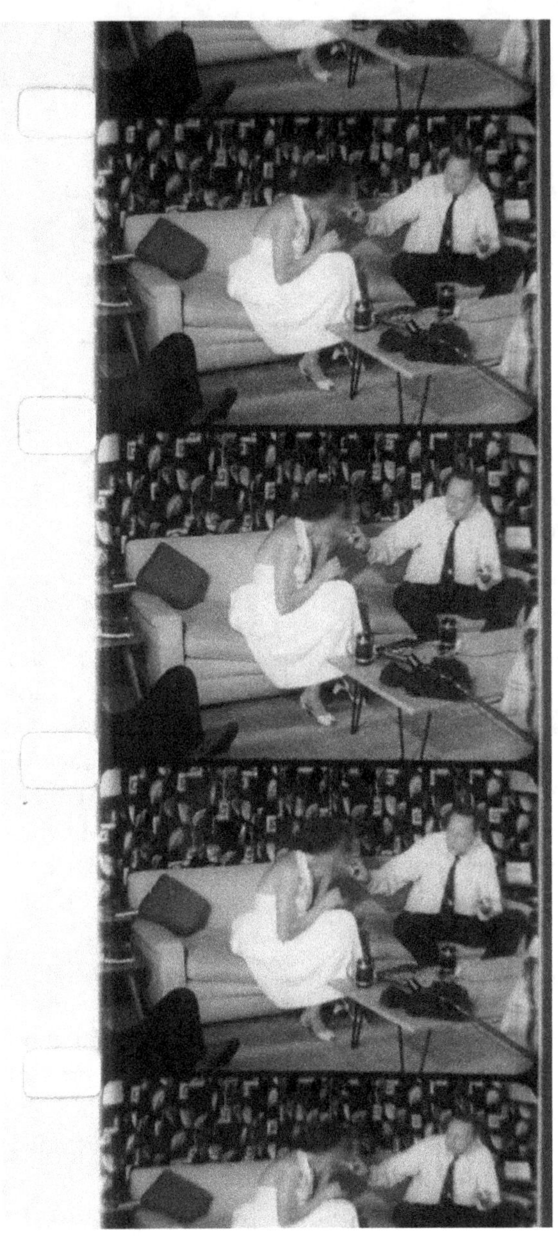

Figure 1.4. *GB-SU-005* or "Doris Film," dir. Gregory Bateson and David M. Myers, US, ca. 1956. Frame enlargement. By permission of the Bateson Idea Group. At the Bateson Idea Group's request, one of the subjects' faces has been obscured to protect anonymity.

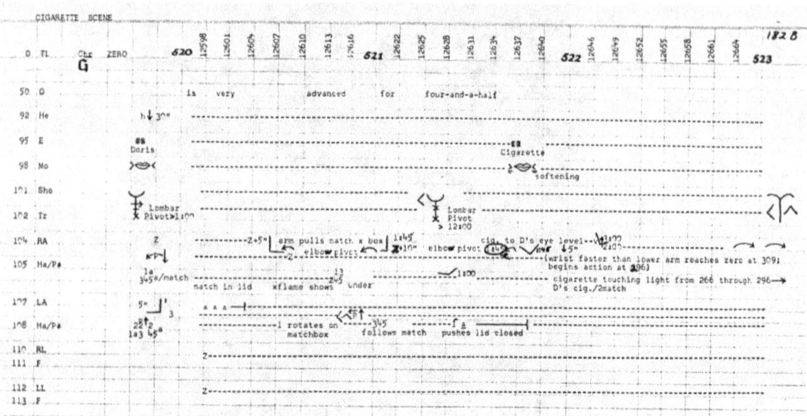

Figure 1.5. Partial kinesic transcription of *GB-SU-005* by Ray L. Birdwhistell. From Norman A. McQuown, ed., *The Natural History of an Interview*, 1971. Courtesy Regenstein Library, University of Chicago.

family, which can also be discerned. When Doris is speaking of her problems with nursing, a marked movement of her shoulder occurs with Billy's exit. It is, writes Birdwhistell, a "startling coincidence."[30] He claims it drew the team's attention to the mother-child bond as a special problem area for reflection and study. Of course, she speaks of her son continuously for all three rolls of film but the coincidence of movements confirms the conflict at a deeper level.

~

Something odd is happening in this analysis. The point is to look for patterns of behavior, not isolated details in the interaction. Yet, a single instance of coincident movement is said to have prompted a whole line of inquiry. Even if all that happens is somehow related, there are strong and weak relations, and this one seems fairly weak. Doris is not even speaking to Billy, nor can Billy see his mother's shoulder move. He cannot see her at all; he faces away from her. If he gets up to leave, it seems far more likely that he does so in response to her verbal complaints about him. Her shoulder may serve to underline her words by pointing to him, the object of her discomfort, but to view that as somehow causing his exit requires the introduction of a new, occult force. One could say that each acts like the limbs of a single organism, though this still begs the question of what it is that binds them. The belief that something does, come hell or high water, is difficult to trace to a theoretical premise. It is even less likely to derive from common sense. A more likely explanation is the form of the instrument the analyst uses to look at these data.

Anyone who has worked with film, and in the process of editing watched a shot countless times, will notice new details emerge with each playthrough—and not only new details, but new relations among them. Things that happen simultaneously now seem to be connected; when they transpire between people they are fraught with significance. The phenomenon can be seen in experimental films that use some form of looping or optical printing. Sometimes it is done for dramatic effect, sometimes for comedy, always with a thrill of seeing hidden things. In any case it tends to gives the impression of figures not just moving, but moving together. Every time the film is stopped and started again, the figures all seem to start up together. They are as if one figure, one organic unit. Their movements are now the joint action of a system. A movement of a shoulder and a movement toward the exit are dispersed across figures yet somehow related. And with each repetition of a prerecorded segment what was seen as contingent, or not seen at all, may now find its place in more meaningful arrangements.

Though the repetition helps, there is some indication that a frame alone suffices. When a frame is placed around a group of some items it seems to perform a twofold operation. By marking off these items from a totality of items, it affirms or reaffirms the unity of what it frames. Typically in photography and by extension, the movies, this frame includes one or more real human figures. And unless subdivided into other, smaller frames, we see it as an image of one time and one space. Its figures are co-present if nothing else. For some this is enough to say they are related. They cannot help but be related, and the frame of the image is the seal of their relation. We see this very clearly in an unpublished text found as a typescript in Birdwhistell's papers. It probably dates from the late 1950s and gives a description of a single still photograph. The photograph, unfortunately, does not survive. It seems to show a street from an elevated position. There are people on the street, going this way and that. They look like illustrations of the "lonely crowd," writes Birdwhistell, and yet

> one thing can be said with confidence. These individual men and women are not free atoms detached and isolated from one another. They are, although largely out of awareness, adapting their behavior to each other and according to patterns implicit in their common culture. There is order and grouping expressed here—not simply the order imposed by the "don't walk" sign, the traffic laws, or the structure of city streets, but order devised from an internalized system of conventional understandings which channelizes, restricts, supports and makes possible intricate social interrelationships. . . .
>
> Starting to the reader's left Nos. 3 and 5 (the short man in the dark suit and the tall man in the light suit) are in an American male height differential dance. No. 3 stands arms folded, leg next to 5 extended in blocking position—as is his left shoulder. This is in mirror to 5's right leg and shoulder. 3 has both hands concealed as he pulls shoulders back in high armcross. 5 has right hand concealed in pocket. Note parallel facial expressions varied only by the larger man's head position which is slightly lowered and to the right. Thus 3 and 5 can both focus on an object in front of them and at the same time "keep an eye on each other"—the peripheral aspects of the eye picking up all movement. This kind of height differential between male strangers is to be regarded as customary caution rather than clear hostility. . . .
>
> At the other side of the picture, 20, 22 and perhaps 25 illustrate a second and equally characteristic kinesic activity—"motion or stance flow." While we cannot determine who assumed the military stance yet the parallel between the young male no. 20 and the woman no. 22, is clear. The similarity of position begins with foot placement (high heels plus background precludes her putting her toes over the curb) [and] is manifest in the hypererect bodies, projected chin and mouth and chin positioning. The analyst is tempted to complete picture of no. 25, only partially shown here, and suggest that he is participating in the dance and is at "parade rest."[31]

That Birdwhistell could discern the mechanics of integration in a single still frame should give us pause. The relatedness of things and especially of people is taken for granted by the natural historian. It is the default mode of his mental set, which the frame of the image helps to maintain. He "is tempted to complete picture of no. 25, only partially shown here"; he is tempted to call significant whatever falls within the frame. Since a photograph is, after all, the fundamental unit of an analog filmstrip, serially repeated twenty-four times a second, what applies to the one applies to all the others that precede and succeed it in a roll of film. And when figures not only stand but also move together, the perception of their relation is almost automatic. Figure A moves a shoulder as Figure B starts to leave. How are they related? What do they mean? Every playthrough of the segment prompts the same questions.

This account of the process is not entirely speculative. It can be checked against Birdwhistell's own demonstrations. One of these survives as an eccentric teaching film cosigned by his cameraman Jacques D. Van Vlack. Footage shot around the world in a variety of zoos shows families interacting with the animals and among themselves. Hence the film's title, *Microcultural Incidents in Ten Zoos* (1971). Its most memorable sequence is arguably one that the filmmakers took at the Philadelphia Zoo. Like all the other sequences, it has Birdwhistell's commentary. "This is one I really want you to notice," he says offscreen. It shows a man lift his daughter onto an elevated platform so that she can look at the animals below. "Father is involved, daughter's out here—watch daughter." She shuffles her feet and uses her butt to tap her father's stomach, just grazing his shirt. "Touching daddy, touching daddy, getting no response," says Birdwhistell. Description then shifts to the father's responding movements. "Fixes his glasses. Now, he points." His wife, standing toward the background with another child in a stroller, signals for his attention. He turns to her promptly. But "watch what daughter does when he reacts." She releases her left arm from the railing and swings it back to full extension until her elbow makes contact with her father's elbow. Twenty seconds have elapsed with the footage at standard speed. Here Birdwhistell calls for the footage to be slowed. The scene is repeated twice, first at half- and then quarter-speed. "Notice the position of father—maternal, maternal position of the hand," although the narrator's meaning is not very clear. "Father moves with daughter's body," and one does begin to notice how the figures draw closer. Then, at the critical moment of the wife's beck and call, "Father rolls his shoulders toward her." But his attention is perfunctory and he turns back to the animals. Now the girl has reached the apex of her movement excursion. Her elbow hits his; she "imprints her father." Her arm is held in freeze-frame for a full fifteen seconds. The scene is played again at the original speed. Then it stops again at the crossing of elbows (see figure 1.6).

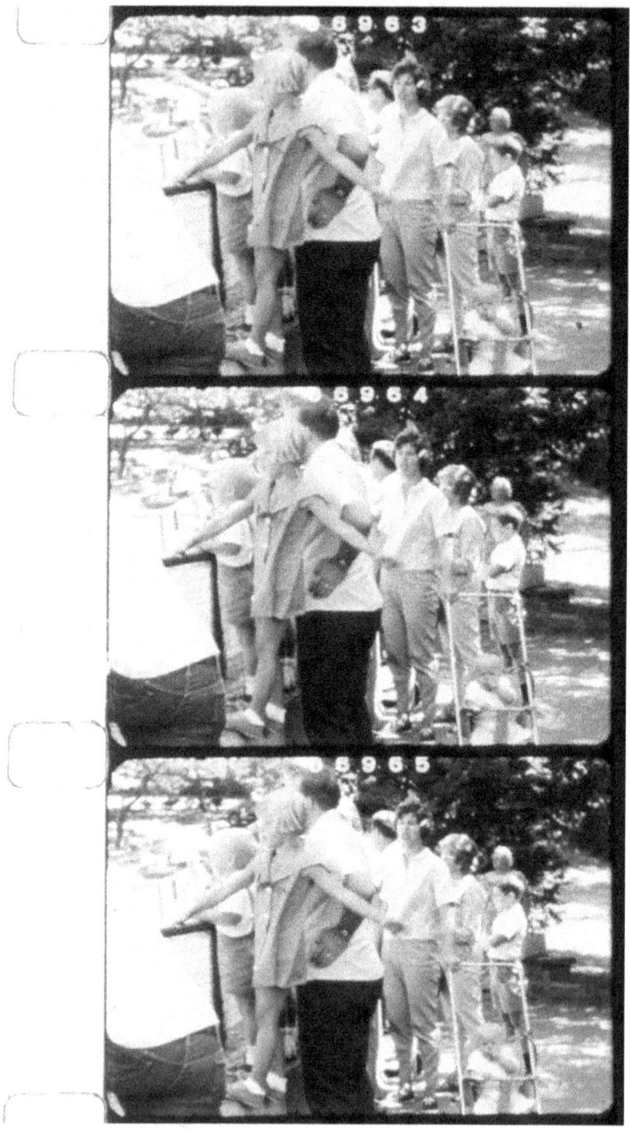

Figure 1.6. *Microcultural Incidents in Ten Zoos*, dir. Ray L. Birdwhistell and Jacques D. Van Vlack, US, 1971. Frame enlargement.

Even in the absence of analysis or explanation, the sheer repetition has its own hypnotic power. Perhaps we are watching the struggle for power than runs through family life in even the smallest details. Perhaps it is an instance of tactile communication. Certainly it looks like an interval fraught with intrigue, mystery, scandal, and even some danger. Still, one cannot help but wonder if what most engaged Birdwhistell was a purely visual detail of spontaneous composition. For the girl's and her father's arms make, when they cross, an X that stands against the maternal intrusion.

The perception is originally of a social relation: of the effort involved in becoming and being human. This is what natural history aims to uncover. It looks at what the organism really does in its environment, with whom, how often, with what variations. Years of work in film analysis start to yield a different harvest, or begin to make explicit an investment that was always there. It is an investment in the picture as pictorial field. The trite metaphor of dance is one clue that points the way. Two men negotiate status through a "dance"; members of the crowd are participating in a "dance." Bateson and Doris have an "interactional dance."[32] Whatever it is that these figures communicate—flirtation, hostility, caution, or the like—they are contoured to one another in formal relations of symmetry, balance, and complementarity. The Doris film proved especially satisfying. It was a thing of beauty one's eyes never tired of. A favorite scene of Birdwhistell's was "the ritual dancelike lighting of Doris' cigarette." He notes the "special cadence," "the batonlike change of pace" when Bateson leans toward her with a burning match—admires "the rhythmic movements of the two participants" who pull in and pull away as if they had rehearsed it.[33] Academic language and special notation cannot obscure his naive delight. In an unguarded moment, he may have even called it beautiful. But this word has no place in his program of research. It has to find expression by roundabout means and even then it must be justified by functional explanations. That "the kinic, the kinemic, and the kinemorphic levels of Doris' circumlexical stress behavior" are balanced against her partner's is just a complicated way of saying that they move together beautifully.[34] That they do this to preserve a social relation is what ultimately justifies the beauty they make, yet their movements have the character of empty formalism regardless. Questions of a mother's feelings, of how often she gives the breast, fade before the glitter of this play of pictorial surface. They seem as if dancing in some obscure way and their dance has no significance beyond relation for its own sake. The human figures dance at eighth-of-a-second intervals; we can even see their footwork when they are framed from head to toe.

Birdwhistell was well aware of his medium's bias in terms of editing conventions that make all talk seem linear. He never stopped to consider the possible bias of the picture plane itself: the relations established by the act of framing. But the more time he spent with the same bits of film, the more his appreciation took on an aesthetic quality. To reckon with life at one-eighth of a second is the most defining feature of his scientific project. To complete the choreography of human interaction is the unspoken feature of his second, aesthetic project. That the pivots and steps seem to grow ever smaller is not a deterrent to the delight that they give. It simply means that even scraps of film can yield this delight for one ready to find it. And if their unity as pictures neither leaps out from image to eye with instantaneous force, nor emerges under the gaze of calm contemplation, but only after each frame is put repeatedly and systematically "to the question," so to speak—the satisfaction of the viewer is by no means diminished. As reward for one's effort, it may even increase.

2

Pictorial (Victor O. Freeburg)

THE PLEASURE WE FEEL IN THE presence of beauty can also give rise to a sense of embarrassment. Most people have, at some point in their lives, stopped what they were doing to admire a thing of beauty. They may even have gone so far as to speak their admiration, either to themselves or to the people around them. There is, it seems, beauty all around us; "beautiful," we say, to confirm the impression. Yet the one who says the word has probably also been told that beauty is only in the eye of the beholder. What gives pleasure to her may make no impression and may even repel the eye of another. Hence the embarrassment when aesthetic judgment is rebuffed by those who disagree, and with whom there can be no argument. The original claim was a statement of self-evidence. Now it is revealed as a statement of feeling—mere personal preference or naive conceit. This state of affairs is very annoying for people who make judgments of beauty for a living.

The word's loose definition only hinders them further. Two philosophers, in 1923, found sixteen different uses of *beauty* in English. It could mean, for example, something enjoyable, but then again it might mean something instructive. Sometimes it names a thing of utility. Since the word means all these things it really means nothing. It is an emotion-word used to trigger nice feelings, and whether beautiful things exist is entirely beside the point.[1]

Some writers met this challenge by trying to limit beauty to a determinate feeling provoked by beautiful objects. If beauty is a cause of pleasure, surely pleasure can be defined as the absence of pain and the experience of wellbeing. Things that do not cause pain, that instead promote wellbeing, would therefore be beautiful in this more objective sense. They are shown to be beautiful from the statistical frequency with which they please people with a standard sensorium. Now beauty is the same for all, now and forever. The proof can be furnished by means of experiment. Pictorial beauty, for instance, will enter through the eye and cause no unpleasure; it will induce a sense of harmony. Its rarefied pleasure is not essentially different from any other kind of pleasure that we might feel. We can see, empirically, which form-combinations give the most pleasure. By showing lines and shapes for different durations, measuring response to stimuli, and collating the results of a reasonable sample, one arrives at regularities and even laws of beauty. Often this leads to formalism in art appreciation, for it is the forms themselves that induce pleasant feeling.[2]

The critic Roger Fry would speak in such terms in 1904 in "An Essay on Aesthetics." There is a universal language of pictorial forms whose combinations, Fry writes, evoke different feelings—evoke them as regularly and predictably as piano keys ring out a series of chords. In gazing at forms we feel physical echoes, and the most successful work will harmonize these. The rhythm of a line recalls our own rhythms, the mass of an object points up our bouts with gravity, while a quality of light can affect us so deeply since light "is so necessary a condition of our existence."[3] The eye moves around a picture and triggers these feelings that, when properly balanced, give exquisite pleasure. It is reported of Fry toward the end of his life that he was "swinging a weight attached to a bit of string above a canvas," apparently to measure the painted forms on it.[4] The laws of form reduce to mathematics and physiology. Yet Fry was never able to explain why people like art whose ugliness should appall them, nor why these people need experts and critics to teach them a language of form they were born with. His task was to convince the public that some works were beautiful based on objective features of their composition.

Victor O. Freeburg faced the same problem when he began giving lectures on the art of moving pictures. Since these pictures had people in them, their figures had to move beautifully to satisfy good if not popular taste. For the audience was full of "badly trained souls" who had to unlearn a great deal to love art.[5]

~

Very few people read Freeburg today, which is not to imply that many ever did. His involvement with films, or photoplays as he called them, was as intense as it was brief.[6] He taught what may have been the first course in film studies in 1915 at Columbia University. He continued to give the course until 1917 when he enlisted in the US Navy to serve in World War I. A serious book-length study, *The Art of Photoplay Making* (1918), was the product of his teaching in those early years. He returned to give the course in 1919 but he left after only one summer semester. The reason for his exit is nowhere recorded, but it may have involved some rivalry with a former student. He went on to sue her on a charge of plagiarism after she used his course material in one of her books.[7] Then Freeburg made one of those mid-career shifts that seems willfully to reject what immediately precedes it. He devoted himself to all matters Swedish. He embraced his Swedish heritage and would serve as the editor of two journals aimed at a Swedish American audience. Still, he managed to publish a second book of theory, *Pictorial Beauty on the Screen*, in 1923.

At that point his involvement with film ends completely. And if his archives are an indication, he was not proud of his work in film. The small set of papers his widow gave to Yale contains no material on cinema at all. Instead we find a perfectly random assortment: papers and slides on the art of cryptography; a torpedo logbook from his years of naval service; a diary concerning a round-the-world cruise; odd, obsessive inquiries into the painter Hesselius; and a very bad play that once featured Sinclair Lewis. We find everything except what would interest us now. It is as if the material was destroyed or suppressed as somehow unworthy of his good name. One has a creeping sense when reading a book by Freeburg that despite his sincerity, he was slumming it a bit with cinema. His aesthetic is utterly classical, his impulse is to classicize, and he prefers the genteel "photoplay" to vulgar "films" and "movies." His first book begins with a quote from Francis Bacon and a facing reproduction of the Venus de Milo.

Freeburg wants actors to act more like the Venus, who has a great advantage by her being fixed in stone. But this classical image of a figure in repose proves hard to combine with the tendency to movement. The films are just too taxing, too ugly as he finds them. Their ugliness arises from the movement of the people in them.

Everything seems to change for the sake of change itself and no one listens to the theorist when he patiently lists their errors. We can speculate that Freeburg suffered from wounded vanity and gave up on the medium he set out to reform. But the most plausible reason for his departure is that he simply grew tired of seeing ugly pictures.

This incidental quality of Freeburg's career in film is as marked at its beginning as at its end. He began at Columbia as a doctoral student and received his PhD there in 1915. His dissertation was published in the same year as *Disguise Plots in Elizabethan Drama*. It does not venture much beyond the subject of its title; certainly film is nowhere mentioned in this very dull book. Two aspects, however, are notable for our purposes. One is Freeburg's interest, perhaps unusual at the time, in the actual presentation of the play-text on the stage. He finds disguise of value because it is dramatic, because it is visual and appeals to the eye, allowing for play with costume and makeup. He seems to conceive of the stage as a picture with a total aesthetic impact going far beyond words. On the other hand, and this is the second point, he does not much like the theater of his own day. He derides the kind of realism found on the Broadway stages; he even blames realism for the decline of the disguise plot. The art of imagination is under an assault that leads not to truth but only "a mess of realism."[8] Thus Freeburg's turn to film seems even more perverse because film is a mess of realism almost by nature. Objects on film can be seen in all their detail, and everything around them is equally crisp.

The incompatibility of Freeburg's ideals and the medium to which he gave eight years of thought is the source of his enduring interest to any student of the human figure. For the figure on film is where the tension is most pronounced; where beauty and ugliness collide in a picture. Whenever the figures move, they unsettle the picture, and in popular films they are moving all the time. That may thrill the eye, but it offers no relief. The result is fatigue for our over-worked senses. Reform of the movies would mean first and foremost that movies move less, or at least in a gentler fashion. When beauty means balance, gradation, repose—first in the object and then in the perceiver—even a lively fire can prove too distracting. How much less beautiful must be the film in which a crook kicks an officer down a flight of stairs, escapes on a motorbike, smashes a cart and fence, and is followed by another car that smashes them up again.

If, Freeburg writes, "you have a sense of satisfaction when you look upon a picture, and if the satisfaction remains when you look upon it long or again, or dwell upon it in memory, then that picture to you is beautiful."[9] It sustains contemplation and it does so by virtue of its careful composition. It cannot be too rigid, it must have variety, but this variety must have order; it cannot be merely varied. It will, as they say, have unity in variety by the design one imposes on pictorial elements. The curve of an arm is echoed in a hill, which leads the eye gently to the curve of a tree, such that one can keep looking without strain or fatigue and without ever leaving the circuit of the picture. The beautiful picture is a no-exit picture, giving pleasure and prolonging it, according to aesthetic theory. And the body responds in some faint degree with a sense of equilibrium, of rest within activity. Each part of a picture must give help to every other to maintain the equilibrium of the viewer's body. To alter one part thus entails the alteration of every other part if the balance is to last. Nothing excludes the cinema from the realm of beauty if only the cinematographer learns to compose with movements. Practically, however, it presents an awesome challenge to those who compose for a popular audience.

If one must have a story, one must also have actors, and if one has actors, then a setting is needed too, as well as such things as canes and hats and gloves, furniture to sit on, and frequently animals. "Thus for any one photoplay the materials multiply until the problem of arranging them . . . is by no means easy of solution."[10] Change within the image makes them multiply a thousand and the human figure is the principal source of that change. Merely stepping to one side can destroy a composition unless balanced immediately by a corresponding movement. And the figures belong to actors, that is to say people, who cannot see precisely the shapes they are making. Hence one moving figure is already hard to manage, two are even harder, and three present a riddle that only a sphinx could solve. The art of animation almost seems preferable, for what it lacks in human dignity it makes up for in control. "Those who exploit it," Freeburg advises, "will be able to teach many a valuable lesson to the director who merely takes photographs of actors in motion."[11] Eight years of grappling with cinema aesthetics lead to this extreme of aesthetic anti-realism. Still he hopes the medium will live up to its promise as the seventh if not the liveliest art.

Used with taste and discretion, film can have beauty; that much is certain for Freeburg the theorist. It might even surpass all the arts that come before it, finding beauty hidden in the stuff of life itself. Its play of light and shadow appeal powerfully to imagination; in it one can contemplate the world as pure appearance. Movement excites the viewer but is tempered by distance. Even "the mob of the market" can be made to resemble a billowing wheatfield when transposed upon a screen.[12] To escape from the mob through art was not a new conceit for Freeburg. It was a lifelong goal and practice, an aesthetic ideal. He had already made it the subject of a poem published in his twenties, with the title "At My Window":

> Below I hear the discord of the street,
> Clatter of hoofs and moan of rumbling wheels.
> The swirling mob a motley hue reveals—
> The priest and courtesan abreast complete;
> Poet and scavenger and merchant meet;
> Scion and gamin tread the matron's heels,
> And over me a cynic musing steals
> Until my temples throb with fever heat.
>
> Then far above I see the silent stars
> That gem the placid majesty of night.
> Sublime and soft they twinkle their delight
> Where no terrestrial sorrow ever mars.
> I soar them and there my fancy hears
> The fabled songs that sound beyond the years.[13]

In the sonnet's first stanza, all the many figures are wanton, unstuck. They merely swirl and swirl, and yet further swirl. The eye of the poet, who endures the offending spectacle, is dizzied by that swirling as he follows its movement. His ears are assailed by street noise, by harshness and "discord," so much so that the word inverts the iambic pattern. "Clatter" does the same at the beginning of line two. The content of the imagery is completely disordered insofar as the mob collapses all distinctions. Here both priest and whore, artist and merchant, legitimate and bastard children must swirl together evilly. They make, as it were, a big mess of realism. The content of the sestet resolves this disparity; it calms the overheated brain of the poet. Now he sees not the street but rather the stars, which seem to him unchanging and thus a place of rest. His glutted eye reposes in their constellated fixity; they allow for contemplation, and they will be there tomorrow. Whatever happens below in the noise of the street is abolished in the firmament with its time beyond time. The eye tours the stars and the soul soars among them. Fever turns to coolness the longer he gazes. It is as if the young Freeburg predicts in this poem the very thing he will seek six years later in movies. Even the darkness that surrounds him is common to both. But the stars on the screen are quite different from the sky's: they are pictures of people, and therein lies the problem.

Thus Freeburg began his work with a heavy load of preconceptions about what was proper or out of bounds for art. He had no obvious passion or expertise for teaching film, and everything suggests that it was something he was tasked with. College life has always been full of contingencies; courses must be filled, schedules juggled. Administration makes use of those who are convenient, which may have very little to do with their achievements. All we can say for sure is that in 1915, Victor O. Freeburg was a recent PhD. He needed to find work, hence he stayed on at Columbia, teaching English in the extension or adult education program. He taught for one semester in his academic specialty before he was rerouted to deal with the "photoplay." No reason can be found, and so we must assume that the arrangement was convenient. Equally mysterious is that Columbia should have offered the photoplay at all as an academic subject. No other school did, and even to see a movie was beneath a gentleman's conduct. Again we must assume that the arrangement was convenient, that it served a strategic purpose in relation to certain interests. There was, in fact, a growing relationship between this university and the early film industry, which then existed largely on the Eastern seaboard. Its producers were coming to the painful awareness that they could not steal plots from bestsellers with impunity. Jesse Lasky and Adolph Zukor, who were still independents, thought that higher education might become another script mill. They hosted competitions, donated scripts and stills, and sent their writers for classroom visits once the Columbia class got started. Several students did go on to have careers in the profession; the class itself was covered and praised within the trade press. For producers there was also the question of how an archive of inflammable nitrate film reels could be stored safely. Zukor specifically had discussed the possibility with Professor Brander Matthews in 1913, and even though it came to nothing, suggestive is that his student Freeburg should teach the course on photoplays only two years later.[14]

Technically, Freeburg was head of the Photoplay Department. In its first year of operation he simply was the department. Despite the apparent randomness of his election, he pursued the task in earnest and with uncommon seriousness. He knew all about plays and much about pictures; he knew what passed for good in the construction of both. He even had some training in the art of paint and brush. Thus the photoplay seems a perfect union of his interests, and if he lacked enthusiasm, he made up for it with principles.

The main principle he offered for photoplay excellence was "significant beauty," the beautiful rendering of significance.[15] The pictures are beautiful and the play-text significant, in the division of labor that Freeburg envisaged. He was, ostensibly, in charge of a class of students aspiring to write screenplays. He had to teach them how to write what is called a good story, but one with some significance, a significant story. He also had to help them write for the movies in particular—for a series of pictures without benefit of the human voice. A picture, he had learned, is supposed to be beautiful. So a photoplay has to be significant and beautiful. Since it has to tell a story, the story should uplift us, and since it has to be in pictures, they may as well be beautiful; hence the criterion of significant beauty. But the relation of beauty to significance is still unclear. There is a gulf between them that the phrase papers over. The gulf widens and widens until beauty for its own sake dominates significance in *Pictorial Beauty on the Screen*. This gulf, and the tension is gives rise to, should always be kept in mind in our review of Freeburg's program. The practical result of his interest in beauty was a strong pictorial emphasis in his teaching of the screenplay. He therefore told his students that they were not writers but "cinema composers," or people who composed in pictures. They would then have to spell out all the details of the picture in addition to the sweep of the narrative line. And they would have to know beforehand what beauty consists of to avoid creating something objectively ugly. Never mind that ugliness might somehow suit the mood. There is no excuse for ugliness because it strains the eye, and if the eye is strained, we cannot get the story. Beauty has at least a functional importance because its opposite, the ugly, makes significance impossible.

Already, in *The Art of the Moving Picture* (1915), the poet Vachel Lindsay had appealed to our need for beauty, and of the two works of theory that had then appeared in English, Lindsay's was the only one to make this appeal with force.[16] The average film is full of "galvanized and ogling corpses," he writes, of "wriggling half-dead men," "rawness and squirm."[17] This is Lindsay's way of saying that people tend to move in ugly ways on film. He is, like Freeburg, an aesthete and reformer; naturally he looks to the older arts for precedent. He asks us to imagine the tomb of the Medicis and to think of what would happen if their sculpted figures woke. They would not begin to thrash, to move by jumps and jerks; their beauty would adhere to them in all their transformations. Actors for the screen would do well to mimic the poses of such figures from the history of art. When posing is mastered, movement can be added so that acting is a matter of poses and transitions. Lindsay admits that the actors play characters; they live, love, and act out their passions. Sometimes they even resort to violent action in the most dramatic moments of the developing narrative. But none of this excuses or justifies the ugly. The actors are "pattern shapes" that impinge on the eye and they should behave in consonance with the canons of art.[18] Hence Lindsay's chapters on sculpture-in-motion and painting-in-motion, as if film could just add movement to the beauty of static forms. *The Art of the Moving Picture* is bombastic, but conservative. It is therefore unsurprising that Freeburg should adopt it as the textbook for his class at Columbia University.[19] But Lindsay's great virtue was enthusiasm for the subject; the rigor of dialectic was unknown to him entirely.

Freeburg was a scholar and also a pedant who was able to make a system out of Lindsay's effusions. The basis of that system is a concept of beauty derived from the aesthetic psychology of the day. It has little to do with the older aesthetic theories, idealist in character, though it shares with them a preference for the same kinds of objects. It gives different explanations for the enjoyment of these objects, explanations rooted in the very nature of enjoyment. When an old master painting is said to be beautiful, its beauty resides in its formal arrangement, which leads the eye gently from one point to another in a potentially endless circuit that leaves one feeling good. The feeling can extend throughout the whole body because other senses are recalled in the process. It is pleasant in proportion to its duration. Extended perception is called contemplation—when the eye looks and looks and never has its fill. "*Beautiful*," writes Vernon Lee, "means satisfactory for contemplation," and it is Lee whom Freeburg quotes in *The Art of Photoplay Making*.[20] Of course, any human figures who feature in the picture will have to be acceptable in this regard. They cannot be ugly in themselves, in their aspect and movement, but even more important they cannot be ugly in combination. They must be arranged in relation to each other so that the whole is beautiful, satisfactory for contemplation.

Though published five years apart, *The Art of Photoplay Making* and *Pictorial Beauty on the Screen* are so similar in content as to form a single theory. The later book is notable for its more strenuous effort to grounds its rules of beauty in empirical psychology. Its focus, per the title, is narrower than the first book. Aside from these distinctions, the books are as one and will not be distinguished in the course of what follows. Let us look at the general precepts, then their relevance for films, finally at their application to the filmed human figure.

All theories, no matter how inductive, still proceed from assumptions we might call absolute—unquestioned, a priori, as the philosophers say. A theory of pictorial values is no different in kind, and Freeburg's has the merit of laying his assumptions bare. He is concerned with two things called beauty and ugliness, where beauty gives pleasure and ugliness pain. Pleasure and pain are physical sensations; they enrich or afflict the body as effects of different stimuli. Almost all people react in standard ways to the stimuli that strike them from within or without. Some things are always painful, others always pleasant, for all peoples everywhere and across the span of ages. One also assumes the pleasure is preferable to pain; therefore beauty is also preferable to ugliness. And the basic empirical test for one or the other is how long one cares to look at the stimulus in question. These, then, are the basic assumptions, but there is still another that is even more basic. It is the belief that the object or picture in question is something we can look at long enough to contemplate.

Not all films are equally fit for contemplation; some even say that film precludes contemplation. It refuses to stay put long enough for the eye to grasp it. The tradition of aesthetics that looks back to

Plato has always sought a glimpse of the eternal in beauty, and the eternal, by definition, does not change its aspect. A verdant plain, a bust of the goddess Juno, even wallpaper patterns can be objects of contemplation.[21] For they are unmoving. There is movement in beauty but it is not in the object; it is movement in the soul of the subject who gazes. Even Vernon Lee thinks so: the "cinematographic succession of aspects" is precisely what she flees when she contemplates mountains.[22] The more a thing moves, the less one can appraise it, until one's means of perception are exhausted by the chase. Beauty would require some minimum duration so that everything can be seen, and seen a hundred times.

Movies, for their part, move all the time, and in Freeburg's day they often moved faster than intended. Too often the projectionist would overspeed the films in an attempt to fit more showings into the daily schedule. They sometimes caught fire as they sped through the projector and burned down the booth, the theater, and patrons. They burned the eyes of viewers in even the best of cases. Then they were gone, replaced once a week by a new batch of films. Rare was the film that stayed on or was revived; most vanished like a fire that is stamped out.[23] The quick change of schedules reflected the changeful qualities of movies themselves, of the medium's properties. Any film, writes Freeburg, "has as much life as it needs" simply by virtue of being a film, and he sought to make cinema fit for contemplation by reducing its fire to a slow-burning ember.[24]

He began to look at stills, not films. Lindsay in *The Art of the Moving Picture* had suggested as much. "Turn to your handful of motion picture magazines and mark the illustrations that look the most like paintings," he enjoins us. "Cut them out. Winnow them several times."[25] If the best is enlarged and framed, and makes a good picture, one can study it further for the key to its success. Then one can make films more beautiful than the average film. Freeburg liked this idea and put it into practice, without having to trouble with scissors and glue. The movie producers who patronized his class provided him with sets of "stills" from their titles. Whether Freeburg knew these were publicity photos is not clear from his writing, but they were sufficiently like the films to function as an aid to discourse. As his collection of stills increased, he placed them in a "museum," in truth an available room at Columbia University. They hung there on the wall like traditional art objects and unlike reels of film that splutter through projectors. A museum, a gallery, fosters certain expectations. It is lit up, not dark, quiet, not loud, and the visitor tends to stand instead of recline. It is a space of contemplation, or at least it can be, when not just a showcase for wealth and prestige. By acquiring stills instead of films, then hanging them in a gallery, Freeburg can look at leisure at what otherwise escapes him. He can contemplate freely. And not only him, but the students as well: they see the stills between their visits to actual museums, thus strengthening the likeness and continuity among the objects. They now look at leisure, enjoy the play of contemplation, and if they watch a film on campus it is not like in the theater. For their teacher can stop the projector himself to discuss some frame or sequence that illustrates beauty. He might set them to write a short work of description with the just-faded images still in their minds. "We discuss the results, and attempt by this method to solve the mystery of visual appeal."[26] They do so in a way that is conducive to contemplation and in a setting, the museum, where beauty historically lives. Theories do not grow in vacuums: the history of ideas is a history of techniques.

To resume, art aims at beauty, and film aims at beauty insofar as film is art. Beauty produces pleasure, delight, aesthetic feeling, of which the negative condition is an absence of pain. Therefore certain things must always be avoided if they give rise to pain, invariably and for everyone. Among the painful stimuli are extreme contrasts of light and shadow, which make the pupils of the eyes expand and contract too quickly. Then there are rapid shifts in the camera's focus, which make the eyes flatten and bulge with each shift. Extremes of color contrast do the same thing. Since the eye follows movement, two opposed movements will force the eyes to cross, and this should be avoided. Suddenness, jerkiness, "pictorial hysterics" make for strain and confusion with no quotient of pleasure.[27]

The concept of beauty contains four different aspects, namely unity, emphasis, balance, and rhythm. Unity has a twofold significance for Freeburg, as there is unity of subject as well as design. A Roman soldier in a skating rink produces no beauty, though it may provoke laughter at its absurdity. Hence there must be, first, a common theme or subject; the contents of the picture must have some form of kinship. Their union is reinforced by the work of composition, which links them together in a field of vision. No line should be so brazen as to hold the eye forever, and where contrast is wanted, it should not be too strong.

There should be gradation of emphasis and the subordination of some things to others in a picture. If a picture pulls in all directions, it confuses the eye; that is the same as saying that the picture is ugly. Emphasis, moreover, produces a higher unity than is often found in external nature. A handful of sand has unity, since every grain is like the others, but this unity is boring because it lacks emphasis.

With emphasis comes balance, the sense of equilibrium—the sense that nothing is too emphatic, for overemphasis destroys a picture. An enormous mass at one edge, with nothing to balance it, makes it look as if the picture might fall to the floor.

Finally there is rhythm, which has several virtues. Negatively it allows for rest in its intervals of silence; positively it moves in repetitive but free fashion. Even static forms have rhythm, broadly defined. The eye feels their percussion as it traces variations in the contours of an object, or as color values alternate.

These principles are familiar because they are derivative. They derive from older arts that define what beauty is and that Freeburg allows to legislate for movies. The newness of cinema is no argument against the old rules, if for no other reason than that the cinema is made of pictures. It is not that the filmstrip is composed of still images—that is irrelevant—but rather that our minds retain a still impression. A thrower throws a disc but we remember his poise just before the release of the disc from his hand. When we think of a runner, we see her mid-stride, one foot thrusting forward and one trailing back. In short, "it is a moment, rather than a movement, which impresses the eye."[28] This seems to contradict the earlier claim that ugliness results from immediate stimuli: no matter, as long as both claims justify classical wisdom. And if moments are always latent within moving pictures, why not prolong them in beautiful tableaux? One could even repeat them at regular intervals, firmly stamping them on eye and mind, giving viewers a place of rest.

Here Freeburg reinforces his appeal to the arts of stasis. He is not unaware that a distinctly time-based art has values of its own. These he derives by analogy from music. All movements in a moving picture should combine like the sounds of instruments in a symphony, "in the same visual key," and each image has its place in a long chain of images that, like a "melody," develops and extends the movements.[29] Thus cinema composition makes equal use of static and fluid forms, one of which is the human figure.

It is useless to protest that one wants to tell a story and that one has no interest in questions of form. "A remarkable thing about composition is that it cannot be avoided," for any object in a frame is already a composition.[30] Infinite possibilities show themselves to people with taste and discrimination and an aesthetic education. They are cinema composers. People without judgment still compose pictures as soon as they run the camera, but they are not composers in the strong sense. They are people who crank the camera, leaving pictures behind them, much as dogs will make mounds while digging in the dirt.

The perfect form of this composition, the model to be copied, is the spectacle of fireworks. Here, "the lines move in similar directions and remain comparatively near together, each one, as it were, helping the others, so that what we see in one part of the motion is a key to the rest of the motion."[31] Other beauties for cinema composers can be found by observation of the things of daily life. For Freeburg they include such beautiful things as curling smoke, the flight of birds, sailboats in motion, moving clouds, snowfall, ice floating downriver, the spiral of an airplane, and the circles produced on the surface of water by an object like a pebble that strikes it from above. These and other motions can be caught and composed, and the result is greater beauty than any found in nature. The smoke that curls up at the left of the frame can balance a waterfall streaming down at the right. The movement of a sleigh curving through the landscape, now right and now left, shades into an image of the landscape rushing past. A swaying field of grain might be placed between a shot of rolling ocean waves and a shot of country hills. If Freeburg had dealt only with pictures like these, his task as a theorist would have been considerably simpler. But his books were contributions to the popular "photoplay," which inevitably meant characters and by extension, actors. Still, he was able to find some films that were not always ugly despite their heavy use of actors playing characters.

Two artists in particular, James Cruze and Rex Ingram, earned special notice in *Pictorial Beauty on the Screen*. Their examples help to illustrate the ideals of theory and bring the problem of the figure into even greater focus. Freeburg was so taken with Cruze's *The Covered Wagon* (1923) that he added it to his manuscript as soon as he saw the film.[32] He also dedicates the book to Cruze "because the various types of pictorial beauty . . . may be seen richly blended with epic narrative and stirring drama in *The Covered Wagon*, a cinema composition that will live."[33] It was produced by Jesse Lasky, an early sponsor of Freeburg's class, but there is no reason to doubt the writer's admiration. *The Covered Wagon* is a period film of a journey west from Kansas to then-unsettled Oregon: a traditionally heroic theme that appealed to his settler fantasies. He himself came from Lindsborg, an old Swedish settlement, and he later wrote a plan to exploit the Peruvian highlands.[34]

Even so, what Freeburg tends to praise is not *The Covered Wagon*'s story but rather the pictures that immortalize the story. The open tracts of country are like canvas to be filled "by the long train of covered wagons, a white line winding in slow rhythm."[35] Soft clouds of dust make it still more picturesque, and the wagons themselves are pleasing with their curved canvas tops. Freeburg notes only the general effect but a look at the film itself may confirm it in detail. The melodramatic segments alternate with vistas in which the pioneers are minified in the immensity of landscapes. One sequence in particular might inspire Freeburg's comments. En route to Oregon, the lure of gold in California gives rise to schism among the pioneers. The caravan splits in two, it divides as it moves onward. In one shot we see the ox-driven wagons cross from foreground to middle as they start to ascend the hill. A dissolve introduces the next image in the sequence, an extreme long shot of the caravan's process of division. The wagons together form a moving, dotted line that splits like a Y at the base of a mountain. One line continues the rightward motion of the prior image and the other line moves left, curving away. They balance the picture by their steady movement to and from the central vertical axis of the picture plane. Their lines echo those of the landscape around them and their rhythms are varied by negative space between the wagons. Another dissolve, another shot, and the wagons proceed past the camera in close-up. They enter from the bottom right corner of the frame and gently arc left around the winding bend. Each shot is not only balanced in itself but its movements are continued and modified by the ones succeeding it. The middle shot, with its bi-directional movement, bridges the movement of the first with that of the third. Thus the picture "adds emphasis to the intense drama of the pioneers."[36] (See figures 2.1–2.5.)

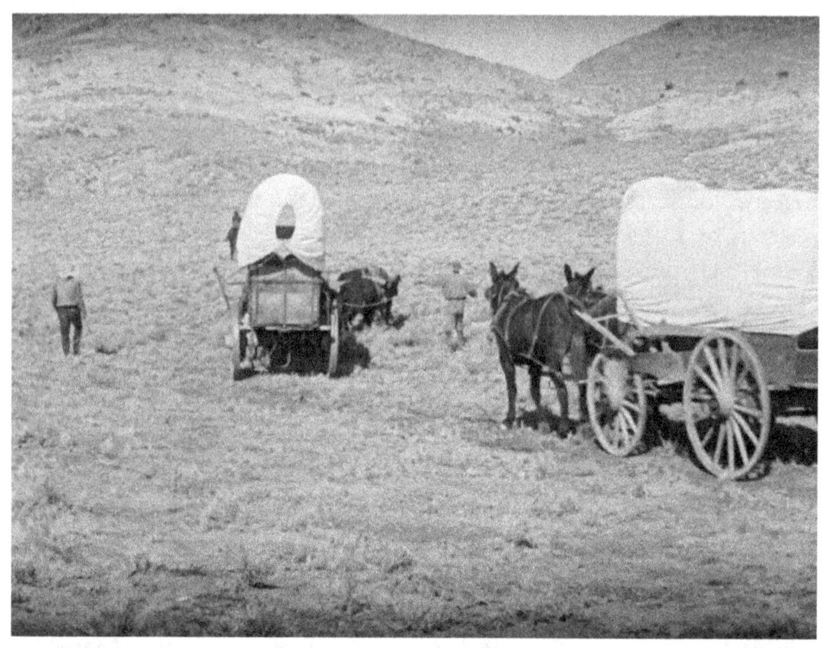

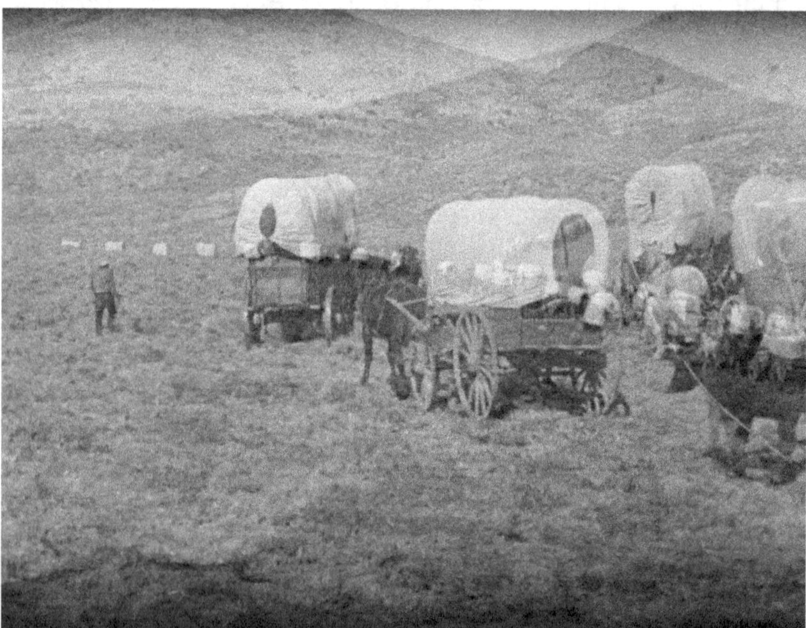

Figures 2.1 and 2.2. *The Covered Wagon*, dir. James Cruze, US, 1923. Digital frame grabs.

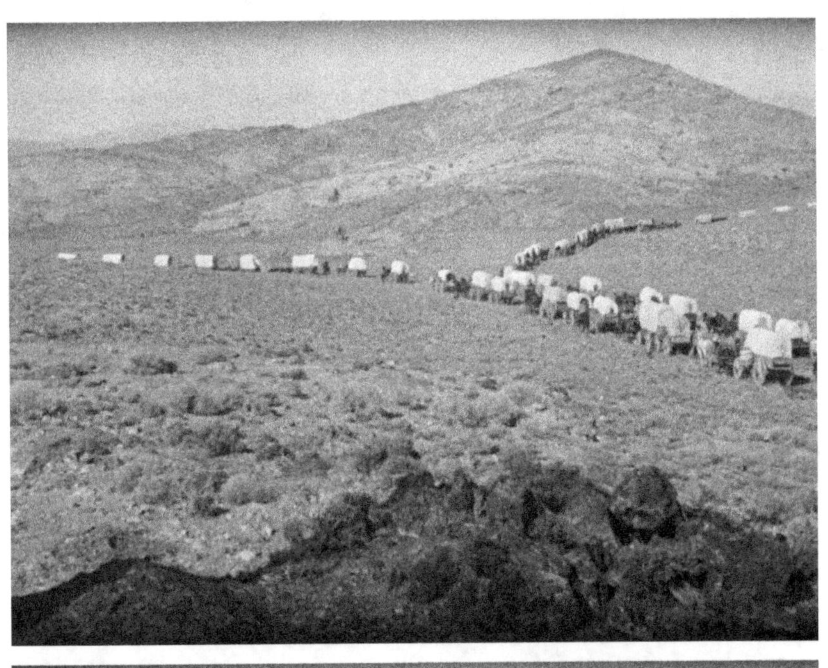

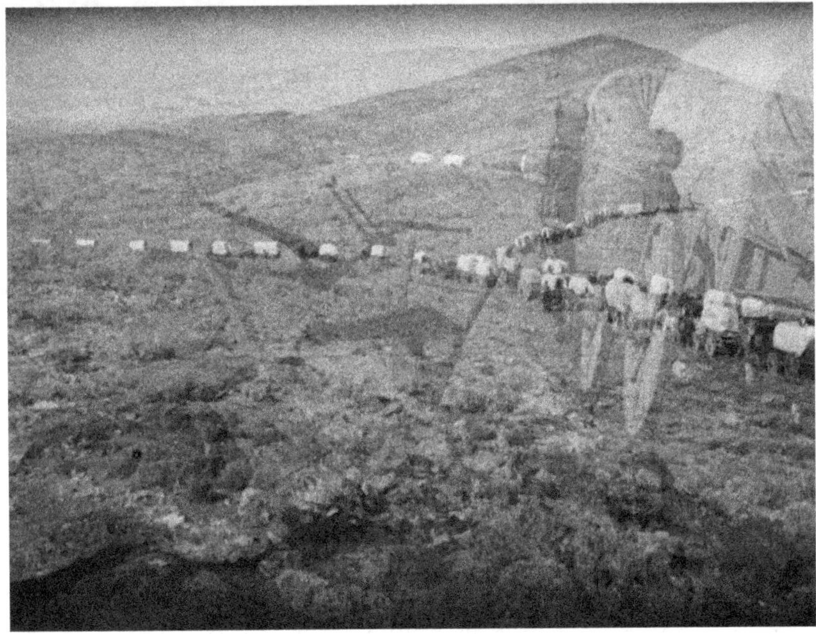

Figures 2.3 and 2.4. *The Covered Wagon*, dir. James Cruze, US, 1923. Digital frame grabs.

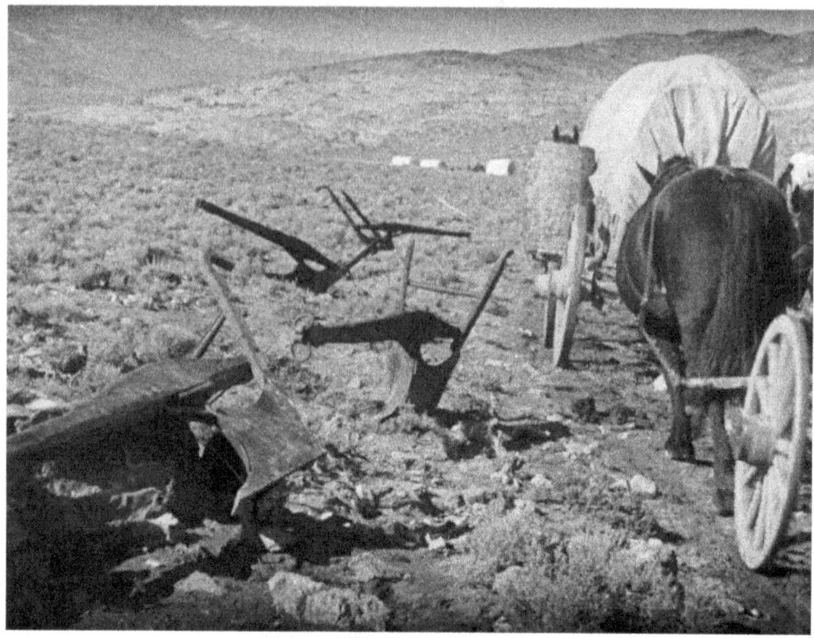

Figures 2.5. *The Covered Wagon*, dir. James Cruze, US, 1923. Digital frame grabs.

But the pioneers are nowhere seen in such beautiful scenes as these. Nor does Freeburg speak of their intense animation while fighting over women or killing indigenous people. We can assume that such things were less beautiful in his view than the line of wagons seen from far off in the distance. Let us try our next example, *The Four Horsemen of the Apocalypse* (1921), whose director Rex Ingram wrote the preface to Freeburg's book. Ingram and Freeburg seem a natural pairing. Both of them were Yale men and self-fashioned aesthetes, and Ingram spoke affectedly of his actors as paint and clay. In this World War I drama he shows the devastation of a small town in northern France. The German army routs the French, then marches through the rubble of the town it has destroyed. Seen from a height and some distance away, two rows of bombed-out buildings converge near frame center. A path runs through that center and winds into the distance. The troops march inexorably from the background to the foreground—as if a snake "had uncoiled itself," to use the language of an intertitle—and they march in a column of three men abreast. The column is also broken by regular gaps that vary the rhythm and give the eye a place to rest. The men tend to follow the lines of the buildings, thus confirming the frame's design, and their movement to the left is balanced by scattered figures around a water well to the right of center. "No undue attention is attracted to either side of this point, but the whole sweep of interest . . . is continuous and even." Foreground and background are clearly distinguished yet also closely bound by the thrust of the snaking line. A central focus is maintained even as the eye wanders off to other points of possible interest. It always wanders back to the moving line. And so the viewer is given something fit for contemplation, "as though war itself were at rest" and could be seen in its timeless aspect (see figure 2.6).[37]

Again the people, the human figures, are hardly there for one to look at. They are there and yet not. They lose all figural quality

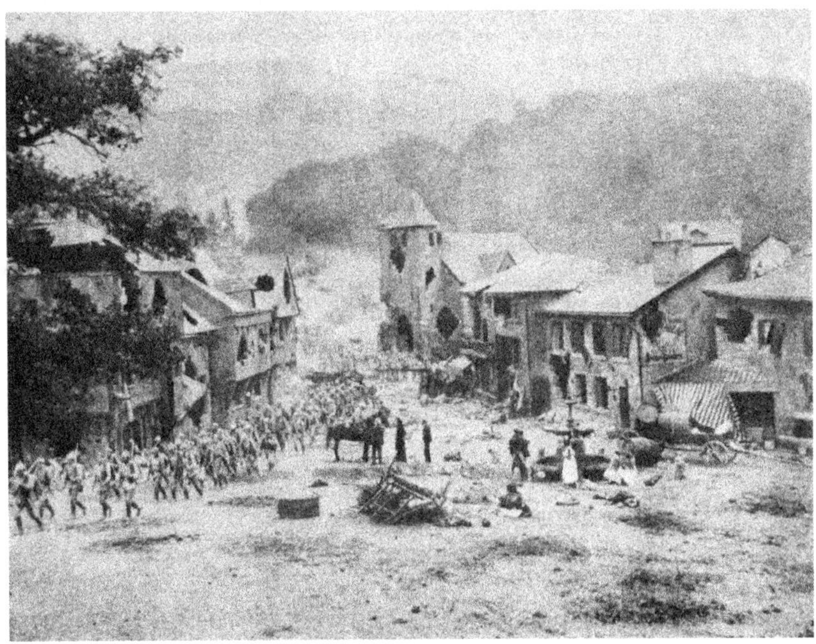

Figure 2.6. *The Four Horsemen of the Apocalypse*, dir. Rex Ingram, US, 1921. Production still. From Victor Oscar Freeburg, *Pictorial Beauty on the Screen*, 1923.

when seen from such a distance and blend together as line and mass just like the covered wagons. Perhaps this is Freeburg's preference. Reduced as they are in scale, they can hardly do wrong; any undesirable movements will be lost in the distance. That is what Freeburg calls "the magic of distance."[38] He is more likely to praise a human figure in the distance than one seen closer up, with recognizable features. But this is not precluded by Freeburg's aesthetics. It is just that real films have no examples he can use. He contents himself instead with speculations, fantasias: examples drawn from films that do not yet exist. When the human figure is seen in all its crispness of outline, and when this same figure happens to move, it can be composed in a way not different in kind from the other shapes and movements that enter composition. The older arts once more furnish the model, for composed figure movement is essentially dance. The limbs of the dancer move together rhythmically while the dancer moves in rhythm with the other dancers. The dance is repetitive but varied, says Freeburg, often tracing a circular pattern around a fixed axis. Each repetition imprints the shape more deeply. The nine muses dance in a circle around Apollo and strike the same poses again and again.

But to film a formal dance is not to film a photoplay; it is only to make a dance film. Nor does Freeburg suggest that the figures on film "should always be shown running around in circles."[39] They should be dancing in secret, dancing in a quiet way, playing characters overtly yet being soft and graceful. Then their motions will be rhythmic; they will be both "at play" and "at work" on the screen. Play is the delight they give to the beholder's eye; work, the drama they enact for understanding. Even a fistfight could be turned into a dance. There is nothing wrong with being natural so long as one does it in an attractive way. That takes practice and judgment. It is much easier and more natural to do things in an ugly way.

Indeed ugliness proliferates at every turn. Take, for example, a woman in a room. She is told to be natural and move about at her ease in the interest of realism, which the audience expects. Yet "she cannot know that to the eye of the camera her nose seems to collide with the corner of the mantelpiece, that her neck is pressed out of shape by a bad shadow, that her gesture points out some gim-crack of no dramatic significance at the moment, that her movement is throwing her out of balance with some other movement in the scene, that her walking, sitting, or rising appears awkward, in spite of the fact that it feels natural and rhythmic to her."[40] She has no idea how much evil she does, has never heard about "the evil which motions may do."[41] Bad movements spring up around her like weeds. They spring up as fast as a composer can root them out. The camera is the agent of a new and astonishing beauty; it also shows how ugly our movements really are. The figure cannot help but add something new to the moving picture; it can never not compose, and this is the greatest difficulty. False is Freeburg's wish "to give the performers full scope."[42] Even their middle range afflicts him with pain. He fears the life they brim with, the ugliness they make; hence performers are really what he wants to tamp down. Their business in the foreground "may spoil a picture," and what they do in the background produces distractions.[43] There are "endless possibilities" of pictorial beauty that arise from combinations of "figure, setting, and action."[44] But the average combination of these is so ugly that the chance of making beauty seems infinitely remote. Troubles are mounting for poor Freeburg's theory.

He takes for a moment the role of the skeptic. "Since the fixed accents [in a film] do not change their positions and the moving accents do, one might suppose that the scene must sooner or later fall out of balance."[45] We assume, for the moment, that the image is beautiful, and that attention is focused on a person or thing of interest. If the figure is in a landscape, perhaps a cow is in the background; if seated in a den, perhaps there is a candle. It is all neat and trim when viewed as a still. Danger arises only when the scene begins to move. The cow starts to walk; the candle, to flicker. Either can pull the gaze, no matter how small the stimulus. What applies to cows and candles applies a hundredfold to figures who must go through the business of telling a story. Even an arm that falls at angles with the spokes of a wheel can easily break the rules of beautiful composition. And if the figure walks across the frame, then the balance is thrown off, and the only way to save it is to pan right with the figure. The larger the excursion of the moving figure, the greater the other changes that have to be made. Figures on film tend to move around a lot.

We began with the phrase "significant beauty," which was simple enough at the level of theory. The figures were beautiful and full of significance, at play and at work: an edifying spectacle. But sooner or later they announce their significance by stepping to the camera and falling out of beauty. They fall out of beauty and into a mess of realism that people, for some reason, pay money to see.

The pictorial human figure is a figure for composition, and therefore is human in a very tenuous sense. To really look at it pictorially, we must leave behind any thought or concern for its needs as a human being. There can be no question of whether its bearer is unhappy, of whether she or he has any motivations. That would only cloud our judgment about its contributions to the whole picture. The figure must be literally emptied of content until only the form remains for our calm contemplation. This emptying out may be an end in itself—beauty for beauty's sake—or simply a propaedeutic to cleanse the picture of ugliness before adding significance. In both cases, though, our compositional sense is sharpened. Things we would hardly notice if we followed the story now leap out to our view as great beauties or uglies. We become more aware of whatever aids or violates our ideas of what makes a picture nice to look at. In Freeburg's case, the ideas are so stringent that he becomes hypersensitive to the violations. The very technique of looking at stills certainly does not help him in this regard. They draw his attention to static compositions that do not exist in the flow of a film. It is hard to believe that an arm at right angles to the spoke of a wheel is really so offensive, especially when their crossing is unlikely to last more than a few seconds before the figure moves away. But the isolated still draws attention to this crossing. It is also much easier to empty the figure of content and significance with only a still. Watching the film itself, we may just be swept away by the motion of the arm as it moves against the wheel. We may not even notice the wheel as an object because our gaze is directed at what the arm is moving toward. There is no direct and necessary link between visual stimulus and viewer response. Rather, there is a focus of attention that makes a film answer to the questions one asks, again and again. The focus creates the very terms of appraisal, the problems as well as their imagined solutions. It can become an increasingly private obsession. One cannot help feeling that Freeburg betrays the popular experience in the interest of his theory. At least, he never seems to realize that much of this ugliness arises from theory and exists for him alone.

But crime always multiplies when the police are present. The criminals, in this case, are the moving human figures, and the worst ones of all are those we call "stars." People paid increasingly to see the big stars in the period Freeburg taught and wrote about movies. With the emergence of the star comes the birth of the fan, who seems to care little for art and aesthetics. The fan wants to know what the stars eat for breakfast, what they do at home, what model of car they drive. The fan wants to know everything except standards of art. In 1919 a cartoonist can depict two women who watch a movie and miss the whole plot; they are too busy talking about whom the stars married.[46] That is not an aesthetic experience of pictures. It is certainly not conducive to the birth of an art, although it may contribute to the growth of an industry. Therefore Freeburg can avoid his theoretical difficulties by heaping scorn upon the stars who monopolize the screen. "The 'star' will insist that he or she be given at least three close-ups in every reel"; "the publicity man insists that the photoplay must be hitched to a 'star' "; "it is the 'star,' " he sighs, "who gets the public."[47] The public may be duped, but not he, the friend of art. He knows that in a masterpiece no star can dwell apart. Judicious arrangement, totality of vision, pictorial beauty "must never be sacrificed to the ambition or vanity of a 'star.' "[48] The stars have no resemblance to true and spiritual beauty; his consistent use of scare quotes points up the ersatz quality. They are nothing like the stars that he saw from his window when he turned his gaze skyward from the great mess below. For when he looks at the screen all he gets is fever heat from the figures who clamor for the camera's attention. His reform of the cinema is wholly unsuccessful and he retreats to the safety of his easel and canvas. Decades go by without a word from him on movies, which now begin to talk, have color, and make billions. "I . . . am pretty much out of contact with my old interests," he writes a friend, "enjoying myself as an artist producing landscapes and portraits."[49] He joins the local art group in his place of retirement. Stars continue to fill up the screen.

3

Institutional (Hortense Powdermaker)

THE WORD *INSTITUTION*, AS Raymond Williams notes, is an instance of our tendency to treat a process as an object. From the fifteenth century on, its meaning slides gradually from one pole to the other. "In its earliest uses it had the strong sense of an act of origin—something *instituted* at a particular point in time"; later it came to name the established customs of a group. By the eighteenth century it often meant a charitable organization, and by the nineteenth it signified anything old.[1] Today we might say of some tenured professor that she or he functions as a veritable institution. We thus equate people with architectural structures, with buildings or institutes, due to their abiding place on campus and patina of age.

The anthropologist's definition tries to strike a balance between process and object, event and solid structure. "The real component units of cultures," writes Bronisław Malinowski, "are the organized systems of human activities called institutions." Religion and marriage are social institutions; they involve people doing things in organized ways. They are processes that go on without very much progress, an eternal return of the mostly-the-same. The people may change, but the form carries over to the next set of people, who have long since internalized the institution's sanctions; for the sanctions are part and parcel of the group's own survival. Whatever organizes people in cooperative action can be called an institution in this broad sense. And the bond that unites them is no mere ideal but is, writes Malinowski, "a material substratum."[2]

Institutions typically have places proper to them. A ritual hut is one place, a law court is another, and a studio for making movies is yet another. One can film almost anywhere but never with the same control as in a well-financed and outfitted studio. It has everything and everyone the filmmaker needs: sets, costumes, cameras, lights, microphones, cranes, and the technicians who make them function. Indeed the know-how of technicians, who know exactly what to do, is as much a part of the landscape as anything else. Even on location, away from the studio, one is struck by how quickly the latter reemerges. By setting up the camera and related equipment, one institutes the studio wherever one goes.

Among the ingredients it gathers together, the actors seem to occupy a strange and unique position. They help to make the movie, but they are also in the movie; they are part of the process still visible in the product. We might even be tempted to treat them as ciphers of the film world in general and of their studio in particular. This is how they appear to the anthropologist Hortense Powdermaker when she travels to Hollywood in 1946. She arrives there in the summer to undertake the study of movie production as an institution. Like Malinowski, who trained her, she defines institutions as forms of activity that satisfy needs—satisfy them traditionally, according to custom. "But," she writes, "there is no simple correlation of one institution to one need."[3] The actor's needs are not the same as those of the film director, even less are they the needs of the studio executive. They are certainly different from those of the viewer who seeks, from the film, a source of diversion. The actor's need is primarily to be on display and, moreover, to show "what he can do."[4] Yet many films fail to satisfy this need. They offer display without room for the display of skill. That is why actors are frustrated, says Powdermaker, who holds a dim view of the studio system. Actors are just the most visible signs of the general dysfunction that prevails within the studio. Writers and directors recede behind the screen; actors are up there, being satisfied or not. Management treats them like "robots" and "serfs" and this treatment is impressed on their films as a result. So Powdermaker argues in *Hollywood, the Dream Factory*, the 1950 book that emerged from her visit. She wants to grasp the human figure in its institutional character, as basically determined by the institution.

The figures she sees onscreen are figures at work and her view of this work must affect how she sees them. But the institutional view of things soon splits in two. The human figure faces outward and inward at once. It lives on the screen, where we watch and listen to it, and in a netherworld of practice that we chart by other means. Our knowledge of practice can sometimes enhance, sometimes obscure what is happening on the screen. It can eclipse the film entirely if left unchecked. Hence Powdermaker's subtitle, *An Anthropologist Looks at the Movie-makers*—for she only discusses how movies are made. But her original intention was to look at the films themselves. "From the beginning," she said, "my hypothesis was that what I found in Hollywood might be related to what I saw on the screen."[5] By the end of her visit, the terms are reversed, so that everything she sees in films is referred back to Hollywood.

The analysis of collective products in terms of group activity is the essence of the institutional approach to art and culture. It differs from natural history in that it does not exclude what lies beyond the frame. Instead the frame is pried open, made permeable to this "beyond." And when we look at the eyes of an actor in close-up, our gaze will now fasten on the arc lights reflected in them.

~

Hollywood, the Dream Factory is one of several books on Hollywood written by social scientists during and after World War II. It is certainly the best one composed in those years. It has seriousness of purpose and psychological depth. It discusses executives, producers, writers, directors, and actors, in that particular order. The order is important, for it adds to the impression that actors are the end point of a long causal chain. Force moves through the chain until it hits the actor like the motion imparted from a foot to a ball. Thus, when the human figure moves on film, it moves under the force of the last foot that kicked it. The portrait drawn by Powdermaker is one of constant kicking.

Powdermaker was well established in the field of anthropology by the time she went to Hollywood in 1946. She had published two ethnographies, one on Melanesia and one on the American South. The second appears to have drawn her to films as a topic of formal scientific inquiry. There were no films in Melanesia but there were in Mississippi, which gave her diversion between her rounds of fieldwork. It was, in a way, a part of the fieldwork insofar as films were part of American culture. She found her new hobby widely shared by informants. They spoke to her of films as extensions of their lives; many perceived a film as just a "slice of life." They imitated films in their talk and way of dress, and the anthropologist made a note of this as a topic for further study.[6]

That was in the 1930s, when Hollywood was at its height. But its study had to wait some five or six years, perhaps due to the crush of working at a small public college. Powdermaker taught at Queens College in New York City, where today there is a building bearing her name. Her efforts began with queries to students, to whom she gave surveys about moviegoing. Then she began the study of historic and recent films, making use of the collections of the Museum of Modern Art. At first she confined her sample to two dozen titles, half from 1925 and half from 1945. Soon she was looking at films from all decades in order to track their changes in content. Authority, conflict, morality, and aspirations were to receive special study in both the questionnaires and films. This is how matters stood when Powdermaker asked for money from the Viking Foundation in 1945.

She met with its director to talk about the project. He was interesting, very interesting, and his name was Paul Fejos. He was an anthropologist and adventurer who had traveled the world. He had also made films in the late 1920s: not ethnographic films, but popular movies with big movie budgets and big movie stars. *Lonesome* (1928) was distinguished as one of the first sound films, and *Broadway* (1929) even had a Technicolor sequence. These films were successful; those that followed were less so, and Fejos left Hollywood over a contract violation.[7] There is no way of knowing how much he disclosed to Powdermaker, yet it must have affected the advice he now gave her. "He told me," she writes, "I could not possibly understand movies as part of our culture unless I knew the social-psychological milieu in which they were made."[8] She flew from New York to Hollywood in 1946, and though she planned for six months, she stayed for one year. Her residence there became a point of pride: she could shame other scholars who wrote of films but did not visit.[9]

She came to see her study as really three books, one of which would deal entirely with studio film production. The second would consist of content analysis, and the third would be a study of the filmgoing public. Only the first was published; the second was announced but apparently never written.[10] Three books on film is a rather large commitment, especially when the first is so poorly received. Few people in the industry were happy with her comparison of Hollywood to Germany under Adolf Hitler. Its reception was equally hostile among social scientists, who doubted the integrity or aptness of her methods.[11] But there are any number of reasons to leave a work unfinished: boredom, for example, or a lack of more to say.

Powdermaker left no field notes to posterity. That is a great loss to the historian. Still, one can form some impression of her research procedure from her letters of the period and her later recollections. Some of her work in Hollywood draws on production files, some on the trade press, but the bulk is based on interviews with about three hundred people. We can see her sitting patiently, drawing out her informant like a good psychoanalyst who lets the patient ramble. She even considers showing them projective inkblot tests. There is no need, however. The people tell her more than they mean to or want to. Some practically denounce themselves while she smiles and nods, in a restaurant or in their oversized homes. Her refusal of a field worker's most cherished tool, the pencil, probably also loosens the tongues of her informants. She is careful not to rush to her rental car outside before she drives around the corner to scribble in her notebook. She talks to John Brahm, the German-born director; to the writer John Collier, who introduces her to others; to actors as different as Alexander Knox and Yvonne De Carlo. All find their way into the rich, composite portraits that make *Hollywood, the Dream Factory* so amusing to read. Aside from this she goes to parties; she keeps her ears open. She attends the movies regularly and looks there for the signs of all the things she has been told. One place she visits rarely is the set during shooting: an omission she comes to regret in later years.

She did go once or twice, at the beginning of her research, if only to see what a shoot was all about. "I was on a set recently for the first time," Powdermaker wrote to Fejos just after her arrival, "and my quick impression was of the importance of the director, as contrasted to the actors who seemed to be pushed around by the former."[12] This impression was confirmed in interviews with dozens of actors. It was also confirmed by what she knew of film history. Surprisingly, she begins her account by saying that actors are unnecessary to the film medium. For film is a plastic art of line and shape in motion; movement is its first and most basic appeal. The forms need not be human, and even when they are, they are easily reduced to an equality with other forms. This is even truer of the silent film period when no voice could issue from the figures we see. So one found ways to make them speak. It was actually fairly easy, as the director was soon to learn. "The director did everything: planned the story, directed the actors, manipulated the camera and cut the film," writes Powdermaker. "'Film Author' was not an inappropriate title for him in those days." He was supreme in his domain. And as his power grew, the actor's diminished, until the latter functioned at the level of props. An actual prop is preferable because it is inanimate, easier to handle and adjust for the camera. "The symbolism of rain beating on a windowpane, the close-up of a hand crushing a letter, two chairs placed cozily by a fire, a large pile of unwashed dishes in the kitchen sink, could be used as effectively as actors, and sometimes even more so."[13] Such images are very useful when the figures cannot speak. But actors had now been speaking—chattering, really—for over two decades on American screens. There seems no reason in 1950 for an actor to be sidelined by chairs, dishes, rain, and the like.

Or at least no artistic reason. People make films for many reasons, though, not the least of which is the exercise of power. Power becomes the principal explanation of what the anthropologist sees and hears in Hollywood. The power to do things or make others do them is indulged in for its own sake by those who run things. It begins at the top with the big-money men, the studio executives who wield power unchecked. Most of them, says Powdermaker, would be equally at home in the front office of a cardboard box factory. They might even be happier since they would not have to deal with such clever and creative people. But he who moves money soon hopes to move more than money, like the wills of his subordinates and the filmgoing public. He may even punish people—directors, stars—whose public success now threatens to eclipse him. He is a big, powerful man whose jealousy knows no bounds.

The producers below him are equally conceited. They are even more annoying because more present on sets. Many seem to have a lamentable tendency to involve themselves in matters for which they have no talent. They exercise power most directly on writers, as a number of common euphemisms then in use suggest. A producer holds writers just like a "lead pencil," and the one he values most will be known as his "wife." Sometimes he puts a whole harem to work, as many as fifteen writers on a single screenplay. Then the screenplay is given to a director who films the stuff, and the film to an editor who somehow makes sense of it. Though directors have fallen from their once-high position, they still exert power directly on actors: "*Do this* and *Do that*" are frequently heard on set.[14] But almost everyone feels the stings and blows of power, and almost everyone can compensate by venting on subordinates.

The actors become a class whose primary function is to receive the stings and blows that burn in the flesh of others. One should not be misled by the size of the typeface that announces the names of actors on movie posters. Actors, stars especially, are the wretched of Hollywood. They are almost subhuman in the eyes of their peers. "It is difficult to find anyone who has a good word to say for them."[15] Their reduction to a status that is something less than human begins with the contracts that bind them to studios. They are owned for seven years; they cannot work elsewhere unless the studio loans them out to some other for profit. The roles they receive are usually repetitious, the better to maintain the actor as a kind of brand. Sometimes the brand is no more than a pair of legs, a silky voice, a hairstyle, a gesture or mannerism. One feels "it would be possible to exchange close-ups from one film to another" without significant damage to the characterizations in either.[16]

These close-ups are suggestive of another reduction, namely of the human figure to pieces of a figure. Hands, eyes, feet, back, these are the items now jigsawed into place. And the director who shoots the close-ups is constantly forcing actors to break off the performance and start up again. Fragmentation defines the actor at all levels of production, indeed it starts long before the cameras begin to roll. Hairlines are reshaped and corsets drawn tightly; eyebrows are shaved and redrawn with pencil. Teeth are straightened, accents corrected, blemishes concealed, and much more besides. The actor is not a body but a set of possible close-ups, a figure apprehended in its dispersal. We always apprehend it in its dispersal, and our institutional concept only sharpens that awareness. The figure appears before us as a many-authored thing—even in long shot, framed from head to toe. Piece by piece we tie it to offscreen technicians. Costumes are by one, makeup by another, sometimes the hair might have its own author. The scenery behind the figure is by the set designer. Light on the figure is the cinematographer's domain. The director, of course, is responsible for the framing that makes it small or big, normal or foreshortened. Emphasis of gaze and voice owes much to the editor. Producers, more distantly, set the limits of variation for the figure from film to film. At the end of the day it seems there is little for the actor to do but show up and stay awake. "In one picture the director gave all his attention in an important scene to getting unusual light effects from a broken glass."[17] Now the actor is merely a prop for the glass, not the glass for the actor, as might be expected.

Of course, "the structure is occasionally bent by exceptionally gifted and strong people."[18] But the anthropologist is most concerned with what is patterned and shared, with what is average in the life of a social institution. Her description aims at giving a picture of the average. The above account taken from *Hollywood, the Dream Factory* purports to show how average films become average.

~

"*The Bribe* may serve us as an example. It is an average feature picture, neither an Oscar winner nor a particularly poor movie."[19] It is, in fact, the only real example that Powdermaker gives. Because *The Bribe* was released in 1949, two years after she finished field work, it received the full benefit of her new vision. Yet her remarks are still meager and we will have to develop them with the hints that she gives us. Robert Taylor and Ava Gardner are the male and female leads; both were signed to MGM, where *The Bribe* was produced. Taylor is a federal agent, Gardner the wife of a man he pursues, in a cloak-and-dagger story of stolen army surplus. Neither star delivers much in Powdermaker's estimate. Taylor is "a weak automaton hero" who moves within the film "passively and without expression." Gardner is slightly better but she seems most concerned to display, for the camera, her "rounded and pointed bosom." Vincent Price is amusing as the chief smuggler; John Hodiak, the husband, passes without comment. Only Charles Laughton is a "really human character," repulsive yet pathetic because his feet are always hurting.[20] Robert Z. Leonard directed the movie, and we now depart from Powdermaker in discussing his style.

Though far from a pure pictorialist, he does have a tendency to slide actors into places where the props can speak for them. There is, for instance, the scene where Robert Taylor considers his options after Laughton threatens Gardner. Perhaps it would be best to let the smugglers go if the woman can be saved and fall into Taylor's arms. Back home, in his quarters, he looks at himself as rain streams down the window and blurs his reflection. The camera pulls back as he turns and walks toward us. He looks up at the ceiling and runs a hand through his hair. He furrows his brow; this means he is thinking. Most of his feelings are given in voiceover, which is curiously flat and in the second person. The camera pans and pulls back to frame him in profile. Now the background can say what the actor cannot. The frame is divided along a diagonal into light and dark halves, with Taylor in the darker. The shadows from a fan's rotation play across his figure. It continues to rain outside; we hear it on the soundtrack. The impression of a man in the throes of moral compromise owes as much to the rain and shadows as it owes to the actor. It may even owe more. The actor assumes a pose, then another and another, in order to catch the values that will give his figure meaning. Emotions are attached to him, not generated by him. The same can be said of Gardner in the following scene when she too is standing near a window streaked with rain. Thus the actors move passively from one scene to another (see figures 3.1 and 3.2).

They move passively through all the spaces of the film institution. Their movement through the film is just a part of their movement through the film studio: there is only one movement. Passivity, writes Powdermaker, "extends to those who work for the studios, to personal and social relationships, to the audiences in the theaters and to the characters in the movies."[21] Sometimes she uses the circumspect language of one thing reflecting the values of another. Characters are passive because they "reflect" the values and culture of the film industry.[22] But very often she suggests a more direct causation. One actor, she reports, "felt like an automaton, making this or that kind of motion, which the camera caught."[23] Such passages imply a collapse of representation into the bare event that the camera records. All films are documentaries if only because they show how people looked on a set under lights. And not only how they looked, but also what they did—how they moved this way and that for the people behind

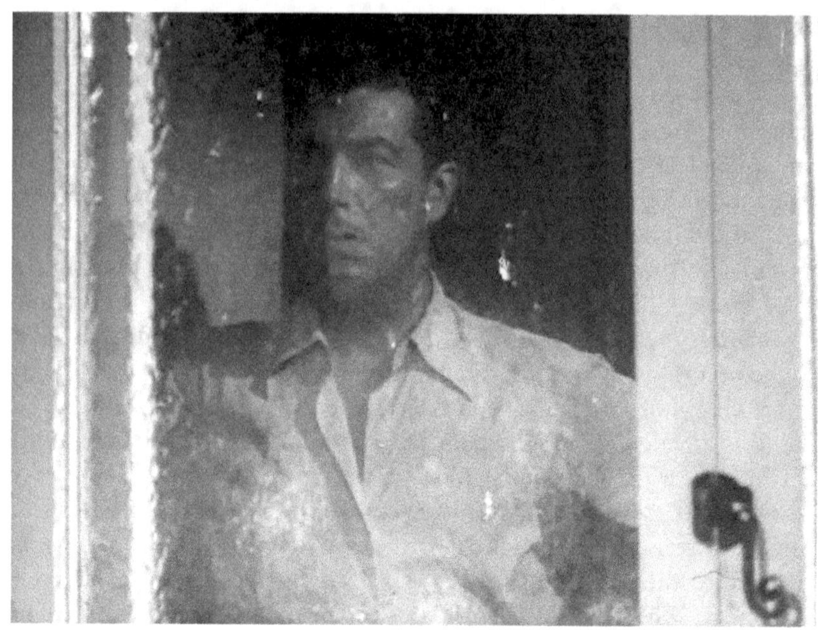

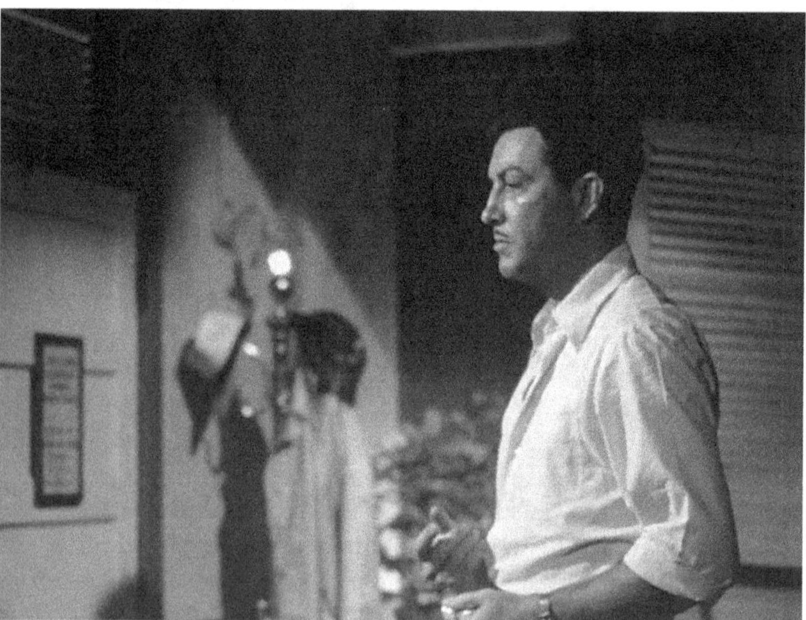

Figures 3.1 and 3.2. *The Bribe*, dir. Robert Z. Leonard, US, 1949. Digital frame grabs.

the camera. Their mortification must be visible because the process of acting is that which demeans them while the camera is rolling. Certainly readers of *Hollywood, the Dream Factory* will be forgiven if this is the conclusion they draw.

The conclusion, and the train of thought leading up to it, can be described as functional in the anthropologist's sense. An artifact of culture, whether a film or a stick for digging, is a function of the needs it satisfies for members. Its function is its meaning, its so-called significance, which can only be inferred from the behavior it supports. What it means is the same as what it does to people, as the meaning of a stimulus is to be found in the response. The functional approach served Powdermaker well in her earliest field work on the island of Lesu. There she was confronted by large wooden carvings and the rituals they were made for, both known as *malanggans*. Even today their iconography is obscure, but it is also the least important thing about them. They might depict the ancestors; then again, they might not; it truly makes no difference for the functional approach. All that really matters is that the carvings function in a chain of operations and a ritual cycle. The cycle begins in summer as a circumcision rite for young adult males—that is, a rite of passage. Older men prepare the carvings over the preceding months, beginning not long after the end of the preceding cycle. When summer finally comes and the boys have been snipped, their elders dance and sing around unfinished carvings. The elders dance and sing again when the painted versions are displayed about six weeks later, still in the summer season. This is an exciting time, an occasion for feasting and promiscuous sex. No woman is ever allowed to see the carvings, which are destroyed in the winter before the cycle begins anew. Thus the carvings can be said to perform several functions. They sustain age and sex distinctions, bring prestige to those who make them, and provoke the exchange of goods and sexual partners. The emotions they inspire last for hours, often days, and then are discharged as further behavior. One does not need to know what the carvings depict to describe the role they play as a social institution. They will only ever have this one role to play because they are junked shortly after the performance.[24]

So too with films, which serve specific functions for the people who make them. But the films are not destroyed, or at least not intentionally. They often circulate indefinitely, far beyond the group that made them. This presents a problem for the functional anthropologist. The approach is further complicated by the fact that movie content is legible to everyone, including the anthropologist. Hokum and illusion deflect the eye from social process. Only those who wield the institutional concept and have enough knowledge to give the concept depth—only they are able to see the film for what it is, a moment in a cycle of need and satisfaction.

Such knowledge can often be gained from other films that purport to show what life in a studio is really like. And some actors lend themselves especially well to an institutional reading of their image or figure. They are usually tragic types, people who suffered terribly and in a public way for many years of their lives. Judy Garland has long been a favorite in this regard, due to her struggles with weight loss and addiction. One writer even speaks of "the kinesics of suffering" in Garland's style of acting as revealed by behavioral science.[25] But this is just a more specialized version of the kind of speculation most people indulge in. We see Garland as a farmer at the beginning of *Summer Stock* (1950), plumper than usual and at home in her plumpness; and here she is again at the end of the film, hollowed out by pills and dangerous diets. The lack of any narrative pretext for the weight loss leaves only one culprit, namely, the institution. Hence we can doubt if she really is happy when she belts out "Get Happy" with her costar Gene Kelly. We can even try collating every scene in the film with an event in her life at the time it was shot—as the recent film *Judy* (2019) attempts to do with reference to Garland's performance in *The Wizard of Oz* (1939).

It would seem that vindication of the institutional concept is contingent on its power to give specific insights: not just general statements to account for "average" films, but particular statements about particular films. At the very least, it should allow us to draw connections between a series of films and their makers' careers. The academic subfield known as star studies is an extension of the concept in this direction. If we know the general shape of an actor's career, we should be able to use their films to fill in the details. A film gives some evidence of satisfaction or its opposite, and the actors are ciphers for the whole institution. They reflect all its values or stand as a mark of shame.

If we now move beyond Powdermaker's great book entirely, it is because we push the concept further than she did. Institutionalism ends in the analysis of stars, whose labor is always visible and cannot be hidden. We choose an actor of the period of Powdermaker's study, one splashed across screens and trumpeted widely. Moreover, we choose a woman, and for the following reason. Female stars and starlets are more obviously degraded by the rhetoric of Hollywood than their masculine counterparts. Powdermaker was not a feminist when she composed her book on Hollywood but her portraits of women are sensitive to their position. They alone face the crucible of the casting couch, and their process of manufacture is more readily advertised. It should be easiest to prove our thesis with a big female star, like the one who was plucked "from the soda-fountain stool."[26]

Julia Jean Turner was supposedly plucked from just such a stool in 1936. She would have been fifteen, playing truant from school. Within a year she appeared with the name Lana Turner in a film produced at Warners, one of the five major studios. After this she moved to MGM, where she stayed for eighteen years, appearing in six movies in 1938 alone. If anyone could be said to be a product of Hollywood, it would be Lana Turner, the girl in the sweater. It was thin and clung tightly, set off by a small black belt. She wore it under the direction of Mervyn LeRoy in *They Won't Forget* (1937), her very first feature. LeRoy made sure the sweater would highlight her breasts and allow them to bounce as she walked down the street. Since she walked with a parade it was easy to sync the music so that her bosom moved in time with the beat of the drums.[27] She made herself known to the world by her walk. Later she recalled her first audition with LeRoy: "'Just walk,' he would tell me. 'Walk from here to there.'"[28] She insisted that her stage name be pronounced *Lah-nah*, while some wits remarked that *lana* means wool in Spanish (see figure 3.3).

She completed the remainder of a high school education between takes, as it were, with other young costars. She often played schoolgirls in those early years. She is the vamp of Carvel High in *Love Finds Andy Hardy* (1938). In *Dramatic School* (1938) she studies at a dramatic school for girls. When not playing schoolgirls, she often played dancers. Sex soon became an obvious aspect of her persona. The "Sweater Girl" had come of age, and a film like *The Postman Always Rings Twice* relies on her sex appeal almost entirely. It was, incidentally, the third most popular film of 1946, the year of Powdermaker's visit. The

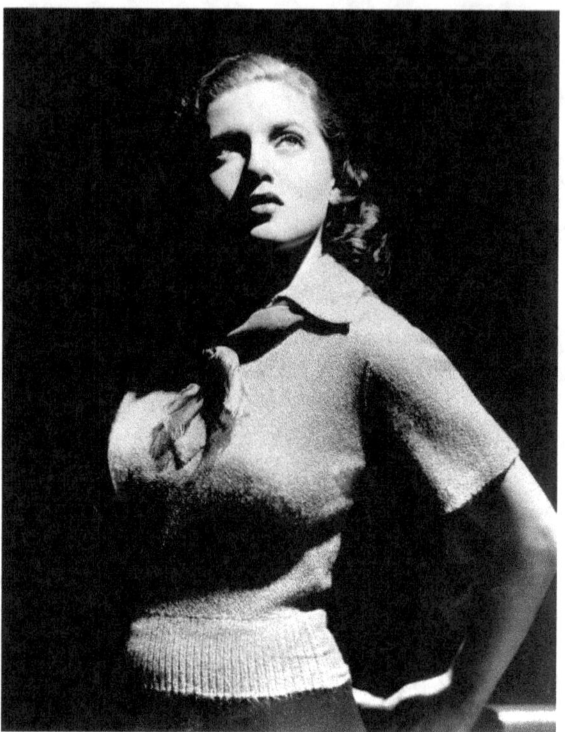

Figure 3.3. Lana Turner. Publicity photo for *They Won't Forget*, dir. Mervyn LeRoy, MGM Studios, US, 1937. Courtesy Photofest.

Turner biography was by then well established. It had become myth, or a twice-told tale at least. Someone discovers her in 1936 *or* 1937, at Schwab's, the Safety Drugstore, *or* the Top Hat Malt Shop, while eating a hamburger *or* having a drink. The drink is either a soda or a malted milkshake; the shake is either chocolate or strawberry flavored. Variation in the details belies their veracity, but surely no one read every profile of Turner. One of the most frequently echoed facts about her is that she has no prior training, in acting or anything else.

Her appearance in *Slightly Dangerous* is a kind of neat summary of the Turner figure in 1943. Bored with her job as a female soda jerk, she throws off the apron and decides to defraud a millionaire. She will impersonate the daughter he lost long ago, whom he misses and seeks through a paid advertisement. Thus she needs a look befitting this position. The transformation is effected when she enters a department store and emerges seconds later looking just like Lana Turner. The temporal ellipsis over a shot of doors revolving has something of the wonder of a machine that reshapes pennies. Such is more or less what Turner comes to mean; she embodies all the charm and chilliness of glamor.[29] There are also less savory aspects of her image, aspects deriving from the sanctioned forms of gossip. Scandals appear with frequency throughout Turner's twenties and accelerate dramatically when she passes the age of thirty. Her failures in marriage, which eventually number seven, are exploited by the tabloids and by her producers. She attempts to end her life in 1951 and this too is reflected in the roles she comes to play.

We might compare all of this with Turner's reflections in the book that she published in her twilight years. She speaks, and speaks often, of the "hard work" of Hollywood. Hard work means rising early for fittings and makeup, press tours and junkets, or standing under the heat of powerful lamps. No mention at all is made of an actor's formal training, although we know from other sources that she was trained. Her idea of a good performance is one that involves a maximum of hard work as she defines it. When she receives an Academy Award nomination for her role in the film version of *Peyton Place* (1957), her response is characteristic: "But I didn't do that much in *Peyton Place*."[30] Compared to other roles, that seems to be true. On the set of *Dr. Jekyll and Mr. Hyde* (1941) the director, Victor Fleming, twists her arm to make her cry. She throws herself down a staircase over and over for a shot in *Ziegfield Girl* (1941) that lasts several seconds. In *The Bad and the Beautiful* (1952) she sits in a rocking car while being sprayed with water from hoses for hours.

The Bad and the Beautiful is an interesting film because it is based in part on the life of Lana Turner. The character Georgia Lorrison lives on the fringes of the movie business in a rathole apartment. There, she drinks herself to sleep. She has tried to end her life on more than one occasion. The daughter of a famous actor, now dead, she haunts the old mansion of the Lorrison family. A fledgling producer (Kirk Douglas) finds her one evening while trespassing on the grounds with a director friend. Years pass, he becomes successful, and he finds her as an extra on one of his sets. He decides to test his powers in a wholly new way; he will make her, a nothing, into a star. He will stalk and harangue and eventually seduce her in order to show the world that stars can be made. So it seems, anyway. Her screen test is abysmal and a director rejects her outright. Nonetheless this producer persists in his campaign. Regardless of her talent, she has a "star quality," which shimmers onscreen and rivets the eye. It shimmers through apparently no effort of her own; one only has to place it in the best possible light.

They set about shooting her first starring role. "The atmosphere," writes Turner, "was totally familiar. The sets were the very sound stages where I had spent so much of my working life."[31] For the film was made at MGM, where she had already been for thirteen years. Doubtless many other things in the film were familiar. Her character rises early for two hours of makeup; a hand draws the eyebrows that no longer grow there. She is fitted for a gown, then asked to walk the room, which she promptly does in an awkward and clumsy manner. "Now turn," says the designer. She turns as instructed. She repeats the walk and turn when the male producer prompts her, and this time her performance is deemed satisfactory. Soon she will learn how to hold a cigarette, the precise angle of the hand and the play of the eyes.

Though her confidence is growing, it is still extremely fragile. She visits the empty set the night before shooting. She wants to assure herself that its lights are not monsters, that the filming apparatus will not eat her up. She steps from the darkness and into a pool of light whose diameter she traces, walking from left to right. There are other pools of light of equal size and brightness and she moves through them successively, as if drawn by their power. She pauses for a moment to survey the machinery. Then she sees a chair that bears her full name. She touches the canvas chairback and soon withdraws her hand. The chair is hers, but somehow not. It bears the name of a star she has not yet become. In close-up we see the volume of space that its back and arms surround in the absence of a sitter. It encloses an emptiness that anyone could fill. The same can be said of the several pools of light that were on when Georgia entered, like traps laid out for prey. They are lights that turn people like her into pictures. Now a nameless fear grips her, and she starts drinking heavily (see figures 3.4 and 3.5).

The star-maker sees that his star needs incentives. Obviously, she loves him, and this can be exploited. He therefore pretends to return her affection, which works fairly well while the film is in production.

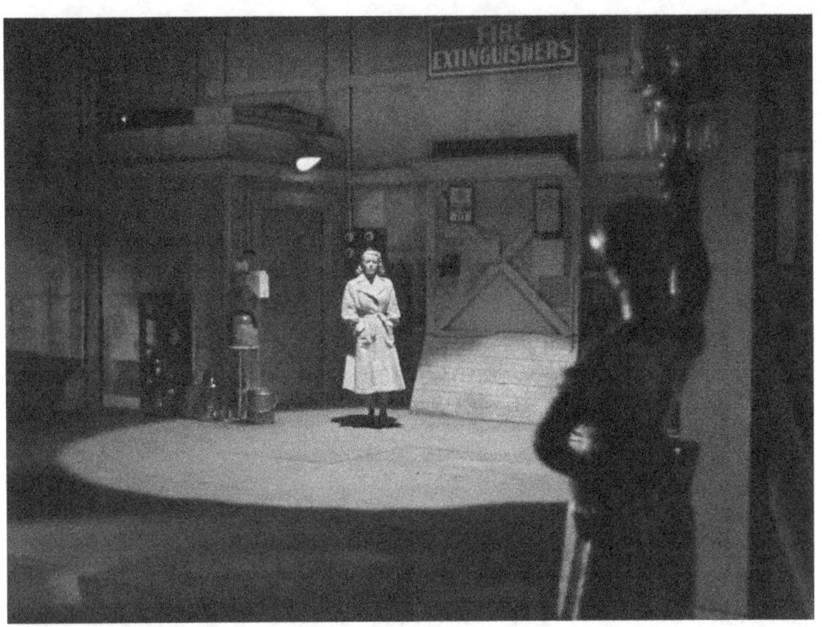

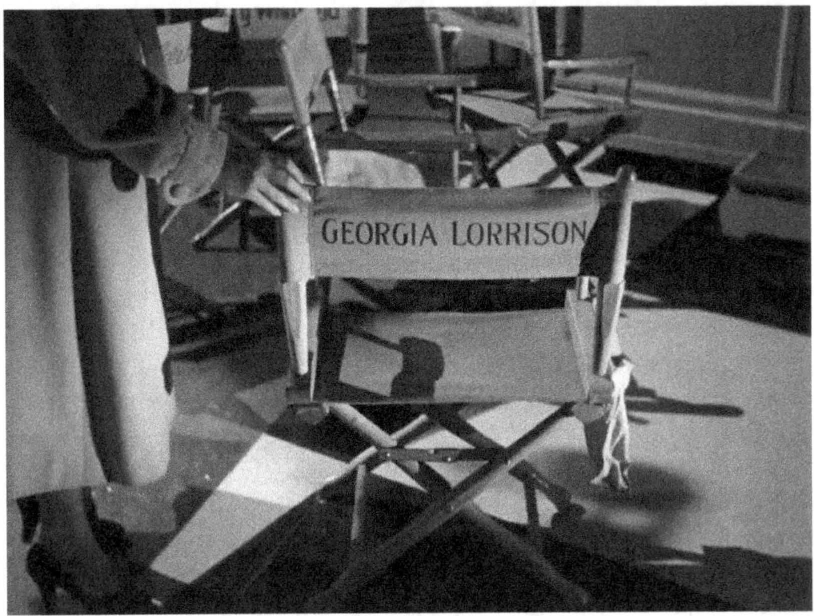

Figures 3.4 and 3.5. *The Bad and the Beautiful*, dir. Vincente Minnelli, US, 1952. Digital frame grabs.

She can play a romantic scene because he is there, just beside the camera, looking straight at her, provoking her performance. The camera records not acting but unshaped emotion that has nothing to do with the scene being filmed. As soon as the shoot is finished he spurns her, brutally, in the foyer of his mansion with a half-dressed female extra. Georgia stands there, inert; it is as if all force has left her. So he gives her one last push through the mansion's front door, which sends her careening in the direction of her car. She manages to find her keys; soon she is driving; sobs wrack her body, and the storm outside is terrible. The camera swings from the front to the rear of the car, then again to the front, miming her agitation. She throws herself back, slams on the breaks and screams as the screen starts to flicker from the headlights of cars. They hit her with the force of photographer's flash; one is tempted to say that she is flayed alive by light. The image dissolves as she slumps against the wheel, and we learn that she became a great success in films (see figures 3.6 and 3.7).

The car scene was a powerful, even overwhelming experience for Turner the actress as much as her character. "After makeup and hairdressing I got into costume and went to the sound stage. There the sight of what they'd been working on all those weeks sent me right through the floor. The chassis of a car, with its trunk and fenders missing, sat on gigantic springs on top of some planks." Nor was that all. "Standing around it was a group of men dressed in the heavy yellow slickers deep-sea fishermen wear. They had big buckets of water, huge sponges, and hoses with fine spray nozzles. Pipes hung from the rafters above the car." Once seated inside, the car began to rock and the water rained down. She tried to recall the emotions of her character in the mansion scene shot more than three months before. "I concentrated on my hysteria, building with each movement of the car." The longer the shoot went on—the more takes they did and the greater the volume of spray from the hoses—the more these emotions of Georgia in the screenplay blended with emotions of the actress who played her. "I went through the scene again, and yet again." The car went to and fro, the rain continued raining, the actress got wet and jostled for a while. "Then another angle. The mike was pushed into the cab, and in my hysteria I sobbed and the mike picked up the sobs. The agony by then was genuine. Too much was coming back to me, too much of my own life."[32] In between

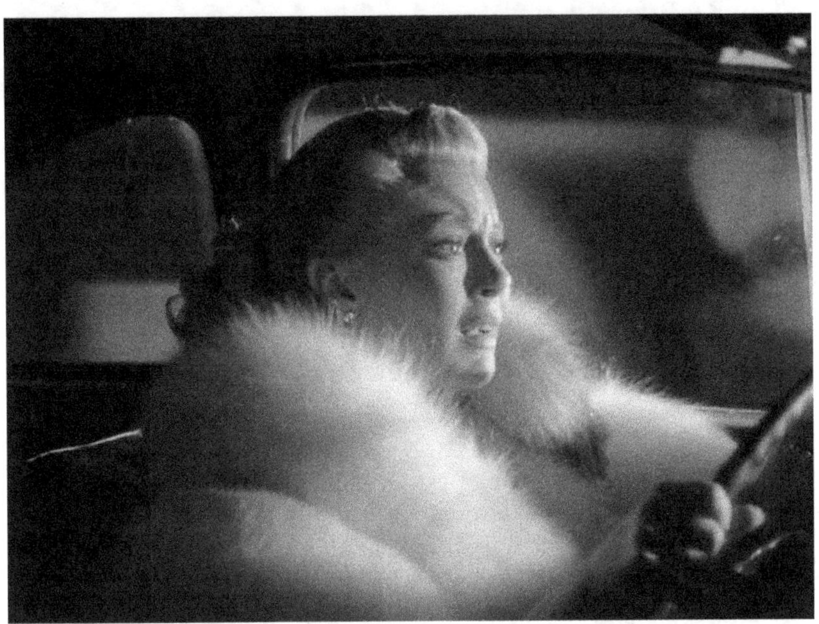

Figures 3.6 and 3.7. *The Bad and the Beautiful*, dir. Vincente Minnelli, US, 1952. Digital frame grabs.

takes, the director kissed her hand. He must have kissed her hand a lot because it took all day to film.

From the institutional point of view, we can see how the film's production informs its final product. The entire institution seems to speak through it. The picture is what it is, the record of a shoot, and the camera reveals an agony that the camera itself elicits. A character has a crackup in a jostling car because actors are jostled both onscreen and off. We watch Georgia suffer, Lana Turner suffer; the two are isomorphic in their quality of suffering. We watch them both suffer under the weight of an institution, and the institutional method would seem to be vindicated.

~

Vincente Minnelli gives a different impression of Turner's performance in the film he directed. It is true that she was often dismissed as a kind of mannequin with no talent at all except to protrude. Indeed that is why he and the writer had cast her. But the popular opinion was "unfair," he writes. One who watched Turner's films of the preceding decade could see flashes of greatness here and there among them. Perhaps she was weak at sustained characterization. You could still do great things with her in a series of shorter stretches. He was not disappointed with the star turn she gave when she came on the set of *The Bad and the Beautiful.* And everyone else was showing "new respect for her ability."[33] John Houseman, who produced, agreed with this and added that the shoot was as smooth as a film shoot could be.[34]

Such accounts could be dismissed as self-serving praise from those who wield power over the human figure. But we might also ask if a person's self-reporting is always a useful index of her or his experience. People tell of what they think they are, or think they should be, as often as they tell of what they really do. It is not that they are lying, for a lie is told deliberately. Rather people fall back on their own self-deception and the stereotyped language that tends to go with it. The reality of their actions may well surprise them. What they tell us in interviews would then be quite useless, or should at least be handled as just more behavior. That Powdermaker sensed this is implicit in her judgment of the Hollywood field work as unsuccessful.[35] She struggled with her own unconscious involvements. Probably the very sight of people taking orders was enough to unsettle her humanist's sensibility. Moreover, her deep identification with a perceived underclass made her overidentify with a culture of complaining. The sheer amount of time she spent listening to people might also have fostered this close identification. Especially without a pencil and notepad in hand, the oral situation allows little distance.

But she never did feel, directly or through interviews, "the genuine excitement which at times pervades the making."[36] Had she spent more time on sets, what might she have seen? Perhaps something like what Lillian Ross will describe in her account of John Huston's *The Red Badge of Courage* (1951):

> With a good deal of zest, Huston then prepared to film the scene in which the Youth comes upon the body of a dead officer propped up against a tree at the edge of the woods. The effect, according to the script, was to be that of a cathedral interior, with the rays of the sun breaking through a thick haze of battle smoke. Huston showed the extra playing the dead man how he should stare open-eyed in death at the tops of the tall trees, and then he showed [the Youth] how he should approach the sight and move back in slow, hypnotized fascination. Then Huston switched back to the role of the dead officer. He seemed to more than identify himself with the characters; the identification extended to the scene as a whole, including the tree. He sat against the tree, his hand clutching his sword, and again the look of death came into his eyes. Quickly he rose and strode back to the Youth's position, and again he demonstrated his idea of how one reacted when one came upon the horror of death.[37]

Such scenes are not untypical of Ross's report, one that, writes Powdermaker, should be "the envy of any fieldworker."[38] *The Red Badge of Courage* was mutilated before release but this has nothing to do with what happened on set.

One could multiply examples endlessly. They would all raise the question of what counts as evidence for the institutional method, which is vague on this point. It works by intuition, with a general impression of how people behave in a given place and time. When it looks at the human figure, it sees something that ties the image to its source in an extremely revealing way. For the film is just a moment of the institutional process, a site where varied interests and personalities clash. A film is a window on a struggle "so intense," says Powdermaker, "that it became the dominant theme of the research."[39] Much of that struggle devolves on the actors who, at any rate, are the ones we really look at. The film records their work in a social institution. That is a fact full of interest and temptation. It might lead us on to the very same fallacy that Powdermaker noted in her early surveys: the tendency to treat a film as just a "slice of life." Only now it is a slice of the institution's life. And as the image becomes a window on the institution, it becomes excessively permeable to the language that surrounds it. Every new bit of gossip comes to inflect it, and every worker on the film has her or his say. Director, writer, producer, star, all can stake a claim to the image's significance. Of course we can always say that they worked at cross-purposes, yet we would only succeed in explaining bad movies.

Aesthetic badness is what Powdermaker tried to account for, but even here we might doubt the form of causation. "Some of the best movies are made by people working together who hate each other's guts": such is the producer's answer in *The Bad and the Beautiful.* It was released two years after Powdermaker's book and feels, in some ways, like a loose adaptation. The ruthless producer, the sidelined director, the writer stolen from the world of letters: all are there in addition to the glamorous actress. But the film functions also as a rebuttal. There is no evidence that anyone involved in its production had contact with Powdermaker or even skimmed her book. Still, one wonders about the screenplay's curious insertion of an amateur anthropologist played by Gloria Grahame. She is in Hollywood with her husband, a visiting writer, and justifies her presence on academic grounds. She is writing a report for her girlfriends back home. She has already lectured on the sexual life of the people who live on a fictional South Seas island. If this is a reference to Powdermaker—the "lady anthropologist," as the trade press often called her—it is a vicious portrayal, for the character is shown to be really quite stupid and totally in thrall to the Hollywood razzle-dazzle. She dies in a plane crash with her seducer, a handsome actor tasked with keeping her off the lot.

The film, nonetheless, has an argument to make. Its thesis is that tensions can be resolved in art by a process of sublimation, or something much like it. This is an abstract way of putting it. The film has no need or use for abstraction. Its characters are its premises and its mise-en-scéne, the syllogism. The producer is a bad man, yet he brings people together. He enables collaboration and the genuine excitement Powdermaker missed in her twelve months in Hollywood. The people who once worked under him are glad to see him fail yet they cannot forbear hearing his latest pitch. He is on the phone from Paris, talking to a subordinate. They gather around the telephone outside the latter's office. First the actress takes the receiver to her ear. Her free hand strokes the cord as she listens to the voice. The two men behind her remain in the shadows. Then the director steps forward and bends over slightly, placing his face beside hers in the field of light. He too is listening. The process is repeated with the writer as well so that all three are together in a sculptural grouping. Consternation, bemusement, skepticism, curiosity pass across their faces, then the picture fades out. The three come together within a single frame, just as all three help to craft the image we see before us.

The image must be judged as a thing within a frame, abiding by rules or laws of its own. And the figures in that image are a part of its texture; they enter its structure and are transfigured by it. Or, rather, they transfigure themselves by transcending the place in which they now stand. They are acting in a fiction, much like she who sits under hoses in a car. "Too much was coming back to me, too much of my own life." We might shift the emphasis here in Turner's statement from "my own life" to what "was coming back." Even if her tears are wrung by the institution, there is distance from the immediate setting, for these tears are based on memories. The experience is transformed and raised to a higher power. It is part of the synthesis effected by acting, by the organization of experience that acting really is. There is, of course, someone in a car, doused by rain from hoses, blinded by flashing lights. But there is more than this car, these hoses and lights. There is acting and fiction; some even call it good acting and fiction. And the figure again exceeds the concept assigned it the more one approaches this threshold of fiction.

4

Fictional (V. F. Perkins)

Fiction admits of many definitions. At its broadest it is simply what is fake or made up. Our own use of the term will be rather more limited; by fiction we mean only a certain way of telling stories. When people say a plot has holes and is therefore implausible, they imply that better fictions would have no holes at all. For the world we see around us has no holes at all. If we grab a piece of concrete and turn it around we do not expect to find a gaping hole, a nothing. We expect to find the back of the piece we are holding. Should we wish to test the realness of the concrete yet further, we can break it into pieces with a mallet or hammer. The inside of the slab should be concrete as well. And if we break it still more into smaller and smaller pieces, without any change in its texture or density, the more our belief in the slab will increase—and by extension our belief in the world it is part of. It has no obvious holes we can see. Nor should the stuff of fiction be pocked with holes; it should give us the illusion of fullness and reality. It should give us a world that is so rich in detail that we sense there could always be ever more details. Between any two details is a possible third that would be there if only the author revealed it. The more details there are, and the more consistent among themselves, the more this world of fiction seems quite self-sufficient. Its density compels conviction in whatever takes place there, despite the better knowledge of our reality-testing faculty. We feel that the artist has not so much created as cut out some chunks of it for our inspection.

This is an ideal we associate with novels, and some would even limit the concept of fiction to the novel as we know it since the early eighteenth century.[1] That is an extreme view, but nonetheless revealing. The early English novel trades on our belief that what we are reading could truly have happened, like Robinson Crusoe scavenging his island. The island has been built up with care and consistency. Its structure is dense; it cannot change whimsically, hence we never really doubt the "solidity of setting."[2] That this ideal now applies even to science fiction can be seen in the premium placed upon world-building.

As for Crusoe himself, he is what we call a character, another word with many meanings but also a normative usage. He tells us about his hopes, fears, and feelings of guilt, in addition to the cravings of his all too human body. Thus the things that he does have meaning or significance. They fall into a pattern. They fit what we know of his psychology and background: his temperament, personality, ideals, and ideology, all of which go to make up his character. Actions without goals are not even actions, and behavior needs a function to be legible at all. For if the characters do things we don't understand, such things become holes in the fiction's plausibility. Indeed the less we understand what the characters do, the less we are sure we are looking at characters. And the less sure we are of this, the less it seems to us like fiction, which is the art of telling stories about characters in settings. Books that have titles like *A Study of Prose Fiction* also have chapters like "The Characters," "The Setting."[3]

The majority of films in public circulation are explicitly fictional in just this sense. Such films give us characters in well-defined settings, and these characters are the focus of the viewer's attention. They show who they are in the things that they do, and whatever they do routinely is characteristic of them. We can hear what they say, hear what others say about them, watch their actions toward others and toward their environment. Sometimes we see into their very hearts and minds and we seem somehow to profit from this curious intimacy. We relive their lives and think the same thoughts in our ever-expanding knowledge of what is possible in human conduct. Apparently our expectations are frequently met, as we bring these expectations to almost everything we see. The desire for characters is so strong at times that we find them hiding out in unlikely places. The famous film by the Lumières from 1895, of a train pulling into La Ciotat Station, seems rather poor stuff if what we seek is fiction. The train arrives, the people get off, and the whole thing is over in under one minute. But early viewers of the footage could see a scheming vagrant in a random human figure milling on the platform.[4] This tendency is just as great over fifty years later, and by then the average movie is more amenable to it.

When three Oxford graduates and their friend from the world of film clubs began to publish *Movie* in 1962, character soon became a major topic of discussion. In its earliest issues we find sentiments like the following: That maturity in characters is much to be desired. That viewers automatically identify with characters and this is a problem when the only option is a bad man. That a recent film of the life of Jesus Christ improves the New Testament by making Judas a rounded character. That the measure of an artist is the measure of his morals as revealed in antitheses of various characters. So natural and pervasive was this kind of language that an issue on documentary calls Hubert Humphrey a "character."[5] Even without explicit definition, the concept of character has several advantages. Characters give to films a certain moral force. They structure narration as a chain of human actions. Perhaps most important, they are a peg on which to hang the many other aspects of image construction. They justify or motivate the other formal choices. A color in the background, an abrupt or smooth edit, a dolly shot or zoom-in might praise or condemn the characters. Then style is the medium of character commentary. Then character flows outward from actor to decor, and from there into lighting, editing, and camerawork. So the film attains a unity, a structural unity that complements the unity of the fictional world itself. Not only are there no holes in the sets and scenery, or in the chain of motivations that move the characters forward; there are no holes of meaning or significance either. The plenum of the visible is bound by the characters who, like God, are in all places and all things. Perhaps the most important idea to be found in *Movie* is that settings are useful as extensions of character.

Movie has always been known for two things, an affinity for classical Hollywood and an approach to classical form.[6] Although its publishing schedule was increasingly irregular, it retained its identity as few other journals did. One finds much consistency among its contributors: a kind of group style, a unity of taste and tone. Ian Cameron, Mark Shivas, Paul Mayersberg, and V. F. Perkins were the editors of *Movie* in its first run. All except Mayersberg had been students at Oxford and published in the magazine *Oxford Opinion*. Cameron studied biology, Shivas studied law, and Perkins was getting his bachelor's in history. They managed to attract national, even international attention for the strident tone that they adopted toward the establishment. They especially railed against British snobbery that dismissed American movies more or less out of hand. Nor did they think England had much to offer in return. Style, they said, is worth fighting for in films; it should be the main object of the critic's appraisal, and there is often more style in an American B-film than in the most committed work of the emergent British New Wave. The British director has no picture sense. He does not even know how to film a setting properly. All he can do is "landscape-monger" dumbly, leaving characters over here and settings over there. Integration of the two is totally beyond him. That was the substance of *Movie*'s polemic in its first editorial of 1962.[7]

The piece was penned and signed on behalf of all by Perkins, the most interesting writer of the original four. They modeled themselves initially on the leading French critics, and Perkins's first publication was in *Cahiers du Cinéma*. Even so, his aesthetic principles are rather different from what one finds in *Cahiers*. A comparison of responses to Nicholas Ray's *Party Girl* (1958) brings out the difference in sensibility well. "*Party Girl* has an idiotic story. So what?" asks someone in 1960 in the pages of *Cahiers*. "But with the regularity of a pendulum, some critics keep harping back to how necessary it is not to neglect the importance of the screenplay."[8] Such a critic was Perkins, who wrote some months later as if in reply: "The moment I begin to deal with [Ray's] methods of composition, or his use of camera movement, I become involved with his meaning." The style of the film is key to "psychological insight," to "characters and relationships," to "the way in which behavior is influenced by environment."[9] Lacking these aims, it devolves into mannerism.

Clearly, mere solidity of setting will no longer suffice. It must explain, reflect, determine, reveal, or illuminate the characters in some degree. The relation between the two cannot be purely formal but neither can it be a relation of mere proximity. It must be something else, something relevant to character: the setting must be an extension of character. How settings can do this when "things change but little, while people change so much" is a difficult question, to borrow a line from Henry James.[10] It is rendered more difficult when one still insists that the world retain its aspect of credible solidity. Hardest of all is when the medium is film, where the background is always present by photographic default. And this is precisely what Perkins demands: that the settings be always relevant, credible, and present.

His demands are not arbitrary but based on certain principles, which one could deduce from a concept of fiction. His major work, *Film as Film: Understanding and Judging Movies* (1972), is an attempt to do just this in a non-pedantic way. The title is perhaps misleading: *Film as Fiction Film* would be much more accurate. Certain films clearly fell outside his conception, like documentaries, cartoons, and avant-garde works. They would need other theories with different criteria. But we can, he argued, understand fiction as the creation of a world in which a story unfolds. The fiction will balance a need for credibility, or internal self-consistency, with a need for artistic order, or expressive significance. These are "twin criteria" to which it has to submit.[11] And if we understand a film under the heading of fiction, then we also have criteria by which we can judge it. We know if it succeeds or fails as filmed fiction.

Perkins, who went on to have a distinguished career in film education, is admired for the depth and penetration of his writing. He is especially good at showing how sequences, moments, and even small gestures provoke complex feelings in sensitive viewers. Yet the range of his criticism is also extremely limited. Scarcely more than half a dozen artists figure in a major way in the pages of his writings. But he maintained that the same criteria used for Alfred Hitchcock would work for many others, perhaps even for most films. The form of the postwar American film "is not," he said, "an isolated freak."[12] It shares generic qualities of the fictional form—with all that the concept of fiction entails. Its criteria essentially derive from the novel, although some would deny the novel's relevance for Perkins. It is true that he was hostile to literary influence; he preferred film as film, per the title of his book. Yet films by his own admission "acquire many of the characteristics of novels" when they are film fictions, with characters and settings.[13] Character is nowhere defined in his work, but its importance is obvious: his aesthetic would collapse without it. In 1960 he tells us we must see *Psycho* twice so that its feints of plot do not distract from the characters.[14] Over fifty years later he structures a book on *La Régle du jeu* (1939) by naming chapters after characters. Actually, it appears that his delay in completing the manuscript was due to doubts about "how coherent" one of the characters "really was."[15] As for the settings, they seem to complete the characters. They ground the human figure in a world we can believe in and they receive from that figure the light of significance.

Stated abstractly, the fictional mode of looking proceeds in the following manner. We begin with the ascription of habits and traits, emotions and psychology to one or more characters. Only that ascription turns the figures into characters. These now form a core, an inner circle of meaning, from which other circles of setting and style arise. Setting keeps the characters from floating in a vacuum, surrounding them with decor and objects and space. Style can further clarify and comment on character. These circles of character, setting, and style are ideally concentric, like the rings on a dartboard.[16] A relationship of nesting has to obtain among them. Their fixity of center gives a rhyme or likeness to each of those circles that take it as their center. And the center, to repeat, circumscribes the traits of characters. Their habits and thoughts and above all their feelings serve to organize images in meaningful ways. Thus a setting evolves into more than a mere container; it becomes a reflection of the quasi-real person, and any and all devices at the artist's disposal can make that reflection more lucid, more poignant. The circle of character holds it all together since everything ultimately points back to character. But if that inner circle begins to develop, work must be done to realign the others. The task of film direction seems to consist for Perkins in this process of alignment at every single moment.

From his earliest writing while a student at Oxford, he tries to find films where the alignment is almost constant. This is a preference shared by others at *Movie*. Sometimes it leads them to strain after meaning, as seen in the questions posed to Vincente Minnelli. "Were the colors (predominantly warm and golden) and the details of the Argentine sets meant to indicate the warmth of Madariaga's personality?" "The candlesticks which divide all these close shots down the middle and separate the characters, are they meant to imply any personal barrier?" "The branch coming down symbolically cutting off Grandfather in the open and blocking Marcelo's path, and the swinging lamp; all this is meant as orchestration?"[17] Minnelli was rather puzzled by most of these questions.

Yet this does not deter Perkins, who brings Minnelli back at a crucial point in *Film as Film*. It is here that the writer begins to develop the parameters of fiction as he understands it. He describes a single moment in *The Courtship of Eddie's Father* (1963) where Eddie and his father prepare their lunch together. The mother of the family has recently died, and it is young Eddie's first day back at school. "Both father and son," he writes, "are making an effort to adjust to their new circumstances." As they move around and touch the objects in their kitchen, the father asks Eddie what he did that day in class, to which the child responds that he wanted to cry. He says these last words during an important bit of byplay. Standing on a step stool, his back to his father, he takes a cup and saucer down from the cupboard. The action of the sequence is entirely believable, grounded in a daily conversation and routine. "The action also takes us graphically inside Eddie's mind and feelings by stressing the instability of his emotional balance." His placement on the stool, his handling of the objects, the rattle of china—all seem to say what the character cannot. The image becomes a single continuum where frailties are echoed in the frailest of things. And even in close-up the CinemaScope ratio ensures equal presence of Eddie and kitchen. It is, in sum, "clearly very skillful as a job of direction."[18] (See figure 4.1.)

It seems to get at something about the nature of life itself, and a look at *Vivre sa vie* (1962) makes this point even clearer. Perkins never cared much for Jean-Luc Godard, and *Vivre sa vie* is no exception in this regard. He finds Godard mannered, undisciplined, and false, and he takes the opportunity to hold the artist's words against him.

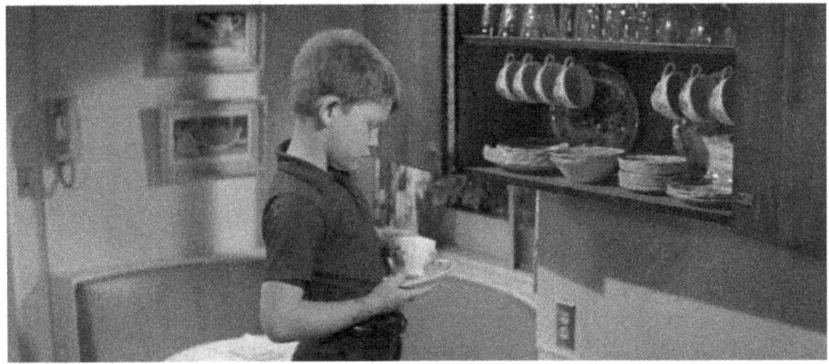

Figure 4.1. *The Courtship of Eddie's Father*, dir. Vincente Minnelli, US, 1963. Digital frame grab.

"Godard has said that his method in *Vivre sa vie* is to strip away the exterior to reach the interior, then strip away the interior to reach the soul. But surely one can only reveal a soul through the interaction of a wide range of exterior effects."[19] Perhaps unsurprising is that Perkins took issue with an extended close-up of Nana's hands, composing a letter. She writes out this letter for almost five minutes and only two cutaways break the fixed perspective. It is effective, in some ways. But to strip the image bare in pursuit of the essential is to block out that setting so possibly rich in feeling.

If Perkins never handled such big words as *Being*, never deferred to any formal ontology, we still sense in this writer some philosophic principle. We might call it his belief that human existence unfolds in a world, and only in a world is it seen to have sense. Hence any film aiming to show that existence will also have to render the world of its unfolding.

~

Charles Barr felt the same, and his work makes an interesting point of comparison. Like Perkins he wrote for *Movie*, if only occasionally. From Cambridge he had followed the *Oxford Opinion* controversy. At first he was scandalized but soon was convinced by their taste and the criteria by which they justified it. His early student writings reveal his debt to Oxford. *La Dolce Vita* earns praise for its use of "environment," which "affects or illuminates the psychology of [the] characters."[20] But *The Entertainer* earns censure because the characters in the foreground "are simply not integrated" with the setting behind them.[21] By 1963 it is an article of faith that "the natural subject for the film is man-in-a-situation."[22] This is more extreme than Perkins, who felt that film had many uses. But if we amend it to say the natural subject for the fiction film, we end up with something quite close to Perkins, and the extremeness of the language that Barr tends to use only makes more apparent a problem they share.

Barr was impressed by the rise of the widescreen process, which all but doubled the width of the old Academy ratio. It helped films to highlight man-in-a-situation. It even, to some extent, forced man-in-a-situation on directors more content with "man + situation," in other words with montage. But any widescreen image tends to hemorrhage its background due to the space that laterally extends.

Even the simple close-up of a head, a hand, a foot, an object will have at its edges some residue of setting. It will have "decor and space and perhaps some casual detail."[23] And with more in the frame, there is less need to edit; the camera can keep on shooting with the rhythms of life itself. "There is no need," Barr writes, "to fragment reality" if one can avoid it by stylistic means.[24] Things have meaning only as they relate to other things, and a film that aims at truth should preserve these relations. A film must manipulate the world through selection but it must retain the image of relatedness in general. Life is man-in-a-situation, not man + situation: its terms cannot be added because they are not discrete. Again we see that Barr is more willing than Perkins to bolster his claims with an obvious metaphysics.

He is more willing, too, to defer to the English novel. He gives the example of *Tess of the d'Urbervilles*, Thomas Hardy's novel from 1891. "Being a writer, he describes things one by one, but they all contribute to the creation of a broad, total environment. His protagonists emerge from this, and are in turn absorbed into it; they are never detached; we retain a mental picture of them as a part of it."[25] Hardy shows its effects on the lives of the characters and especially on Tess, the novel's main character—who, being a woman and poor, is more easily depicted as an outgrowth of the soil.

Barr imagines what would constitute a faithful adaptation. He refers to the scene where Tess tells her husband that she is no virgin and is actually a mother. He does not reply at first, but the room around them does: for "the complexion even of external things," Barr quotes, "seemed to suffer transmutation as her announcement proceeded." Nothing has changed, and yet everything has changed. "The fire in the grate looked impish—demoniacally funny," while the metal grate "grinned idly, as if it too did not care."[26] Nor does the water bottle come to her aid. Barr recommends a continuous full shot to the director who chances to film this event. The couple, the fire, the grate, and the bottle should be visible together as the change passes over them. Separate close-ups of each would be far too abrupt, and in any case, with widescreen, one does not need them. To film Tess in close-up would be like uprooting a flower from its bed, then pressing it for an album. It would be Tess + situation, not Tess-in-a-situation, and what applies to the one applies to all the figures. "I can't imagine a better method," writes Barr, than to film from a distance "without any overt emphasis."[27]

His argument is appealing, but his confidence is misplaced. There is no reason the setting should seem at all different. Without any change of lighting or even a change of angle, it will continue to stubbornly be what it was: namely, a room. It is not more expressive just because we see it longer; it may even become less. Indeed it is more likely to proclaim its irrelevance as the changes in the characters become more pronounced. The irony of Barr's example is that it shows Tess when she is willful and decisive—when she acts most like a character. One might even say that only now does she emerge as a character in the strong sense, standing against her setting. We thus return to the concept of fictional characters, who, unless simple, are bound to develop. And if things change but little, while people change so much, they change even more when we see them on film. They are changing all the time, from moment to moment. The more volatile they are at the level of emotion, the more difficult it is to motivate background changes. A setting that always covaries with character is in danger of dissolving like the play of a kaleidoscope. The novelist solves this problem by omitting the background when, for the moment, it has served its end or purpose. In the words of one writer, "the background may fade."[28] It can and it must periodically fade. But what is used here as metaphor would be literal on the screen. The background would fade and leave the characters stranded; they would stand in front of nothing, their world having vanished; and our belief in their story would fade just like the background.

It is good to be expressive with the elements of fiction. Yet the expressive must remain within confines of credibility and it is this, writes Perkins, that "remains the controlling factor."[29]

Although *Film as Film* has been described as "Romantic" or, worse yet, "Romantic parody," it is really less Romantic than realist given its emphasis on credibility.[30] Its author sees no value in a world so created only to be changed and changed again at the artist's convenience. Such work he deems lazy, lacking in rigor. When a film lays claim to fiction, it must show some restraint; one has to create a world and then to respect it. Texture, density, and resistance to change are key to the illusion of fictional closure. The settings must persist and so constrain what is possible, for their inertia is truly a part of their realism. One must build not a stage but "an apparently solid world" where some things can happen and some simply can't.[31] This world is in process but is never so changeful as to assume, out of nowhere, a wholly new arrangement. It is peopled by entities, human or otherwise, who are also solid, determined, and to some extent predictable. Its laws, its physics, its hardness and resistance, its impact on lives and their impact on it, all give to any world its power and cogency. It must resist even the caprices of its maker, "must obey its own logic," as Perkins writes.[32] It is not different in kind from the world that we know. It is, however, raised to a higher power, is "more concentrated and shaped than that of our usual experience."[33] And one must always be careful to shape without misshaping because the expressive slides easily into bombast.

Even good directors sometimes forget this. A case in point is the example Perkins gives from *The Criminal*, the film by Joseph Losey from 1960. In one scene in the prison, during a convict's monologue, all the lights are dimmed except the key light on his face. Darkness surrounds him and the horrors he tells of. He addresses an audience in the prison cafeteria, but no guard or prisoner turns down the lights. Even if someone had, the result would not resemble this strange illumination with the face alone lit up. Such devices have the benefit of shutting out distractions, a benefit outweighed by the sudden loss of realism. A camera can freely reframe its objects but a setting cannot be freely relit; for the lights are still a part of that fictional world which elsewhere has been so solid and regular. And the viewer is not given "an acceptable reason for a change."[34]

Where Losey subtracts, Sergei Eisenstein adds. He inserts things in his films with no regard for dramatic relevance. In other words he forgets he is making filmed fictions. At the end of the day, writes Perkins, *Battleship Potemkin* (1925) is still the story of a mutiny. It has for its subject neither Marx nor dialectic but "the experiences and feelings of a group of rebel sailors." The ship is their basic setting, then the sea on which it sails, and finally the port in Ukraine where it docks. Presentation of their hardship has been strictly realistic, despite some fast cutting and an aggressive use of close-ups. Yet the director feels free to drop into a battle three shots of stone lions rising in protest. The error lies first in the lions' absence from the actual setting where mutiny occurs, and second in their absence from the lives of the rebels inasmuch as those lives have so far been disclosed.

Meaning is imposed; it should arise from within. If in *The Courtship of Eddie's Father* a teacup is a teacup before it is a symbol, here the lions are symbols before they are statues. There is no particular reason they should even be lions instead of "crashing waves, lightning storms, threshing machines and so forth."[35]

Perkins offers another method for bringing forth meaning, one he thinks closer to common experience. At first, he writes, "décor derives its meaning from character and action." It soaks up some aspect or aspects of character by means of a metonymy that seems to unite them. A style of dress, a way of behaving, a social connotation, maybe even a certain color can remind us of the place from which a person comes. The setting retains all those aspects of character and duly recalls them each time we see it. It retains, that is, the life one sees lived there. The question then arises as to what extent a setting creates, rather than contains, this life one sees lived there. It is closely bound up with the fates of its characters, and their behavior in turn is partly its result. It is now "charged with meaning."[36] And the tighter the fusion of figure with background, the less we tend to ask who or what acts on whom.

Surely Hitchcock could be trusted to know "the power of his decor." In *Rope* (1948) his procedure can be seen at its purest. The film starts in an apartment when Brandon and Phillip murder a friend from prep school with a length of rope. They then stuff his body into an old chest, which they later repurpose as a rude buffet for dinner. They have guests due at seven, including the dead boy's father, his society girlfriend, and another friend from school days. They have also to reckon with their schoolmaster, Rupert, who once enticed them with notions of murder as an art. He could thus be accused of a share in their crime. In any case the film seems to turn on the principle that murder will out, and this affects the setting. As the process of detection comes nearer its goal, it is joined or even presaged by changes of setting. Not that one setting gives way to another, for all the action is confined to this three-room apartment. But somehow the setting changes in aspect while also adhering to the strictest surface realism. The light fades down to darkness in the course of the party, so gradually "that we *sense*, rather than observe, the nightfall."[37] The setting itself seems to grow smaller because we see less and less of it as the film goes on. First the dining room drops out, then the connecting hallway, until "we are confined to the sitting-room only." There is still enough room for the killers and Rupert to arrange themselves in triangles, giving shape to the guilt they share. The camera, furthermore, involves us in their lives by miming their emotions with its tracks and pans. It has the swagger of Brandon, Phillip's hesitation, "the tentative and fearful probings of Rupert." Tension mounts until it bursts in the form of revelation. When Rupert opens a window to signal for help, "one can almost feel a gust" come into the apartment.[38] All this is made possible by the presence of setting, its persistence in time, and its fusion with the figures for whom it is the hangman. There is also a neon *S* seen flashing through the windows, and though Perkins does not address it, one could say it looks like rope.

We should, in fact, say something along these lines to preserve the setting's relevance for fictional characters. The expressive must be made to mesh with the credible; the two must overlap in one self-same setting. It is true that any film is pulled in two directions, "one towards credibility, the other towards shape and significance." But a great film approximates "total cohesion."[39] It is so for any fiction, in any artistic medium. Movies, however, present an extra difficulty. The director is unable to blot out the setting even when it is irrelevant to anyone's feelings. Of course, one could just blot it out, but then one would sacrifice the greater share of realism. And a setting is likely to wax and wane in relevance as the characters change in the course of a story.

At a fairly basic level one can think of a character as having one, two, or *n* characteristics. One can also then imagine one, two, or *n* different settings that correspond to this set of characteristics. And as the character moves inevitably from one place to another, the setting can be keyed to the prevailing characteristic. Nicholas Ray was especially good at this. *Johnny Guitar* (1954), a favorite of Perkins, shows Vienna split between her masculine and feminine sides. Her two-story building, with her business below and her lodgings above, corresponds roughly to that split in her psyche. Downstairs is the bar with its mostly male patrons, from whom she takes refuge in her upstairs apartment. The latter "with its more delicate, feminine décor" expresses all the feelings she denies herself downstairs.[40] The two are linked by staircase, and as she shuttles between them she displays her range of character. Otto Preminger also knew how to map traits of characters. The singer Kay in *River of No Return* (1954) is split between desires for looseness and stability, embodied respectively by a gambler and a homesteader. Since the first man is associated with a saloon and the second with a general store in Kay's town, and since these buildings stand facing each other across the street, her inner conflict is staged as she walks between the two.[41] Down, up, masculine, feminine; back, forth, vice, probity. But this can only cover the grosser shifts in character. One also has to work at a finer grain of detail.

Perkins asks us to consider the following scene from *Carmen Jones* (Otto Preminger, 1954). Joe escorts Carmen to a military prison but is blocked in his purpose by Carmen herself. Her whirligig nature disturbs his stolidity, and she is determined to steal him away from his sweetheart. His disgust for this woman soon becomes real attraction, and two shots seem to mark the point of transition. First the pair is seen frontally through the windshield of a jeep; the jeep in turn constitutes their physical setting. Because the windshield from this angle coincides with the widescreen image, the bar that divides the windshield also subdivides the image. On the driver's side is Joe, with Carmen beside him in the passenger seat. They too are sundered by the vertical bar. Behind them we can see a country road in rear projection as the many trees that line it recede into the distance. Carmen sidles up to Joe to fondle and tease him, crossing the visual and symbolic bar. He tosses her back. She puts her feet up on the dashboard and starts to sing a tune about café life with its dancing and drinking. Then she climbs into the back seat, putting her arms around the driver, who tries to wriggle free while watching the road. On her line "I oughta have a sweetie pie," the film cuts to a side view of the speeding car. We see it now truly as an open-air vehicle, no longer enclosed by the geometry of the windscreen. This, with its vertical bar, has been pushed beyond the frame. With Joe to the right, intent on his driving, and Carmen to the left as she sings and harasses, the landscape rushes by in a blur of brown and green. "Remarkable in this short sequence," writes Perkins,

> is the way that character, ideas and states of mind are projected visually without compromising the credibility of the image. The first shot begins as a graphic expression of Joe's personality. It shows us his world as he wishes to see it—a world of order and stability. But as the shot develops

> we see that the order is rigid and inhibiting, the stability unnatural, claustrophobic and rather lifeless.
>
> Where Joe submits, Carmen challenges; the latter part of the shot gives us her view of Joe's world. She rejects external restraints; demands license to act according to her own needs and impulses. She makes a brief effort to assert her freedom within Joe's structured world, by exploding the neat symmetry of "his" composition.
>
> In the second shot she has given up the attempt. We are offered a picture of her world, and a direct contradiction of the previous image. This world is open, vigorous, fluid, but also chaotic and essentially aimless. There is plenty of movement but it exists for its own sake, to satisfy a restless craving, without direction. Preminger's camera extracts full value from the scenery's flashing passage, but we never see where the jeep is going. The framing of the picture cuts off our view so as to deny the suggestion of a goal.
>
> The contrast between the two images summarizes the conflict between Carmen and Joe; but the development of the sequence, carrying us from Joe's world into Carmen's, conveys also Joe's mounting involvement.[42]

If we think of this scene as a set of concentric circles consisting of character, setting, and style, we can see that the three are tightly aligned. But they are differentially so across the pair of shots. Each has its own direction and magnitude; each has a vector that flows through the circles. In shot one it is centripetal, for Joe appears as turnkey in a jail of his own design. He has totally submitted to a rigid discipline that presses him down and determines his actions. With the shift from Joe to Carmen comes also a shift in vector. The movement becomes centrifugal, flowing outward from a center. It is as if her emotion travels on a song to impregnate the landscape and then change the camera's angle.

If the angle did not change in accord with her feelings, then, by implication, the circles would be nonconcentric. They would only overlap—which is also to say that any shift of vector, any marked change of character, requires realignments to hold the whole together. And since alignment is a process, the disorder will last until this process is complete. So the circles must shift all at once, en bloc. Only then is their constant mutual relevance assured. Of course, the setting itself could change along with the characters. It would not be a credible setting if it did. For when it can be bent to the moods of one character, it is not the common property of all a film's characters. The secondary worlds that all create around them cannot destroy the one world they share. Luckily, any setting is varied. Carmen can enter Joe's world, and Joe can enter hers. But when we stop to consider how many such shifts must occur over the course of the average feature film, we are likely to regard these two shots as exceptions. Indeed, as soon as Carmen's song is done, the setting falls into neutral and is just a country road (see figures 4.2–4.4).

Characters need settings to achieve credibility; settings must be solid to seem credible at all. Characters exhibit changes in the course of narration, some more than others, often at different rates—and a setting could alter in line with these changes were it not first debarred by its need for credibility. Therefore, a credible film with changes of character is in danger of having its backgrounds made null.

Perhaps this is why Perkins, when asked what he looked for, said he often started with "moments of stillness."[43]

But films, with few exceptions, are more than just a series of moments of stillness. Between those pregnant moments lies everything else. When Eddie is done with his teacup and saucer he leaps off his chair and runs to the door.

In the great film, writes Perkins, "no question arises whether the camera moves to accommodate the movements of the characters or the characters move to justify the movement of the camera . . . whether the décor takes on meaning because of the action within it or whether it is the décor that makes action meaningful."[44] But, inevitably, such questions do arise. We have now to consider what viewing conditions would allow this type of question to really be heard.

We have mostly been dealing with the logic of a concept. But any method of study involves some interaction of technique and concept. We know that a film is viewed, and that we can view it in quite different ways—with whatever techniques we can or prefer to access. Perkins's first studies were made under conditions of theatrical

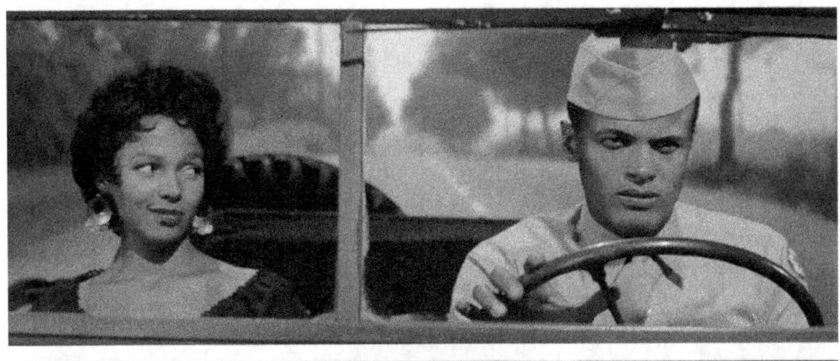

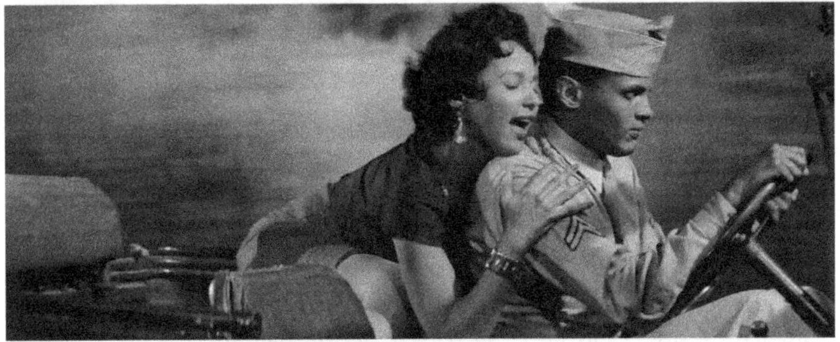

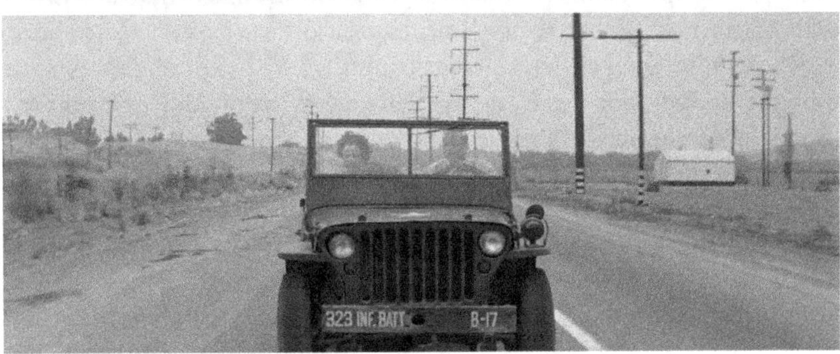

Figures 4.2, 4.3, and 4.4. *Carmen Jones*, dir. Otto Preminger, US, 1954. Digital frame grabs.

projection, like any paying customer. He could not stop or rewind or slow the film down with those home-viewing gestures we now know so well. At best he could screen it two or more times in sequence, and the same went for most of his colleagues at *Movie*. They took notes in darkness to the best of their ability, and whole monographs were often prepared in this fashion. So one went to see movies; one duly took notes; then one wrote essays with the help of one's memory and the quick observations scratched out on paper. Sometimes one consulted the work of other critics. A few frame enlargements or publicity photos could further help conjure the film one had seen. In special cases one might question the filmmaker directly on a point of technique or the import of a symbol. This set of operations defined advanced criticism when Perkins began his work in the early 1960s.[45] It raised normal filmgoing to a disciplined practice by concentration and reconstruction, that is, by imagining.

What we call imagination is a good filler-in: it fills in the gaps in what we perceive. If something partly blocks my view of the street, I imagine the street continuing behind this obstruction. There is no reason to think otherwise based on my knowledge. Psychologists speak of object permanence, philosophers of imagination: insofar as both fill in, they are functionally identical. They aim at a real description of things and events. My missing piece of street is neither real nor unreal; it is simply unavailable, and so it is imagined. The act is no different from that of the historian who imagines Caesar's journey from Rome into Gaul, on the basis of good evidence that he was in each place successively. In this imagination differs from make-believe, which falsifies deliberately for either fun or wish fulfillment.[46] If we thought imagination gave rise only to error, we would not respond to stupid questions with "Use your imagination."

Still, it is not direct perception, which retains the possibility of correcting its mistakes. Perception explores its object one facet at a time, and through that exploration discloses new relations. There is thus a lag of time between perception and knowledge as one runs to catch up with the wealth of perceptions—and all the more so when these are in motion. Hence, the really careful scrutiny of any film object requires apparatus that can slow it or stop it. The standard tool for film scholars was the flatbed editing table, so named because its purpose is to help the film editor. It is a big, complicated, expensive machine and is typically the property of large institutions. It allows both for playback at normal film speeds and for manual alteration of the speed at any time, including the ability to stop on a single frame. One can run the film backward, forward, backward until one is satisfied that everything has been revealed. It was likely Perkins's efforts in film education that first gave him access to such a machine. The editing table was a fixture at Bulmershe College and, later, Warwick University.[47] "The rewind lever," he recalled, "freed the work from dependence on the hazards of memory."[48] He was aware that this machine might yet harbor its own distortions. To repeat or to pause is to give a new emphasis; to give a new emphasis is to make a different film. So he cautioned film analysts to always check results in light of their experience of a film when seen normally.[49] He cautioned, that is, against loss of that holistic vision that played no small part in the development of his theory.

There is, nonetheless, a change in his interests after the completion of *Film as Film*. In 1972 he admits that great films are still burdened by things "whose sole function is to maintain the narrative," but he believes that such pedestrian, necessary evils can be constrained within the limits of a film's early sequences.[50] For as soon as the setting and the characters are given, they can ramify and blend with more or less rapidity. They can then remain cohesive for the film's remaining run time, and any segment one ponders will reveal that cohesion. Or so it seemed to Perkins, for nothing had yet forced him to see what lay between the most pregnant moments. But this can hardly be avoided when one's hand is on the rewind.

Perkins wrote no second treatise after *Film as Film*. Effects of the new technology are to be found only in the ever-increasing detail of his descriptions. A 1982 essay on *Letter from an Unknown Woman* (Max Ophüls, 1948) can serve as our example, coming as it does after a nine-year hiatus. Not only does it read like a shot-by-shot analysis, by then a standard hallmark of academic rigor. It also deals with a sequence—the so-called Linz sequence—of which the crux is one character's noninvolvement with setting. The character is Lisa Berndl, a Viennese woman at the turn of the twentieth century. She is in love with a pianist, also from Vienna, who once met her briefly but scarcely knows that she exists. Her romantic hopes are dashed when she is forced to move to Linz. There, she nurses her passion and fantasy in private. Publicly she tries to conform to social dictates. Her parents arrange her marriage without much delay, and on a Sunday she is taken to meet the man who courts her. This young lieutenant greets her with military briskness before propelling her mechanically through the streets of Linz. She is awkward and skittish with him. If the scene gives an impression of "extraordinary unity," it cannot be discovered in her sympathy with setting.[51]

The scene consists of sixteen shots. The first three depict her walking with her parents to greet the lieutenant before going into church; of these the second shot is a close-up inserted in an otherwise continuous crane shot from afar. Hence we see the characters totally surrounded by the bustling banality of the city of Linz. We do not see inside the church; a dissolve signals only that service has ended as the company pours back out into the square. The fourth shot shows a bandleader conducting his band as Lisa and the lieutenant make their exit in the background. They walk to the nearby park. In a fifth shot they sit on a bench within an alcove. From the sixth through the twelfth they hold an abortive dialogue, either in two-shots or shot-reverse-shots. In the thirteenth, fourteenth, fifteenth, and sixteenth they return to their families, who are watching from a distance. "Where other episodes in the film are of immediately striking brilliance," this five-minute sequence "appeared to be excellent in a straightforward and rather marginal way."[52] That is what makes it such an interesting challenge for an aesthetic of total cohesion.

There are things in the background one could relate to characters, if one was inclined to, out of habit or need. When Lisa and her suitor sit down in the alcove, the frame reveals behind them a wrought-iron fence. Since bars, doorways, and other frame-like enclosures were often taken by critics to stand for entrapment, it would be tempting and logical to call this fence a prison. Then it would express the two figures' repression, their mutual alienation summed up by the bars behind them. But Perkins takes a different tack. He gives the iron fence no symbolic weight at all. For him the setting has just a limiting function and is notable chiefly for not being someplace else. "It is a hard little alcove which offers no means of evasion."[53] It locks people in place, and in them it fosters some words and behaviors.

Perkins announces the theme of behavior when he first notes the bearing and posture of the figures: the lieutenant's smugness, Lisa's passivity, the rigidity of his father, the punctiliousness of hers. Their behavior is derived from "social institutions" of class, military, marriage, and sex that animate this world of circa 1900. That Lisa seethes beneath the surface is really quite secondary to the social interlock of that surface itself. No objective correlative betrays her thoughts and feelings, no part of mise-en-scène points up the inner life. There is only her behavior as it mixes and clashes with adjacent behaviors in the surround. Her "dejected submission," for one, "is pictured not just in the costume—with a hat that seems to be wearing her—but in the awkwardness of [her] movement." And the lieutenant's true nature is to be found in his gait, in his ridiculous ramrod posture, in convoluted sentences that supposedly speak of love. The setting, meanwhile, "is entirely exterior and ostentatiously irrelevant to Lisa's emotion."[54] To look now to the background would be to miss the point. The cause of the behavior is in another person; it is social and immanent to the given context.

"These points," writes Perkins, "are borne out in a further element of the film's gestural vocabulary: the use of hands." His discussion is long but worth quoting at length, if only for what it tells of the new mode of looking. The setting seems to vanish behind this play of hands. Lisa's "never leave her lap, at most twisting there in resourceless agitation." The lieutenant, for his part, "has command of his gestures, to such an extent that he can silence Lisa . . . by peremptorily raising his stiffly gloved arm." There is, however, an air of the hobbledehoy about him, and after minutes of fumbling he receives his rebuff. The time has come to save face. "He terminates the conversation by rising (in one movement, like a released Jack-in-the-box) to salute her and then extending his right arm to her with a disjointed 'Oh . . . then . . . please!' as his sense of correct procedure asserts itself over his confusion."[55] Meanwhile the parents misread this as success. They enjoy that illusion as he begins to rise. When the camera returns to the bench for a final shot, we see Lisa on his arm—because he has offered it (see figures 4.5 and 4.6).

In short, the characters are seated for a significant duration. The camera often frames them within the same shot. Hence one can see how a gesture is made and how it is registered in a reaction. The man stresses points with his baton-like use of hands; the woman wrings hers, desperate to leave. The woman tries to speak; his hand urges silence. She confesses unwillingness to marry this man; he rises abruptly from the park bench. He proffers his arm; she rotely accepts it. And these are but the grosser movements one might observe.

The work of V. F. Perkins began as an attempt to identify the means by which films express character. Along with this it made claims as to which films had done so, and how well they had done it. But with a change in technique also comes a change in emphasis, a new field of observation for the student of film. And what does he find there in a length of filmstrip, in the intervals that lie between

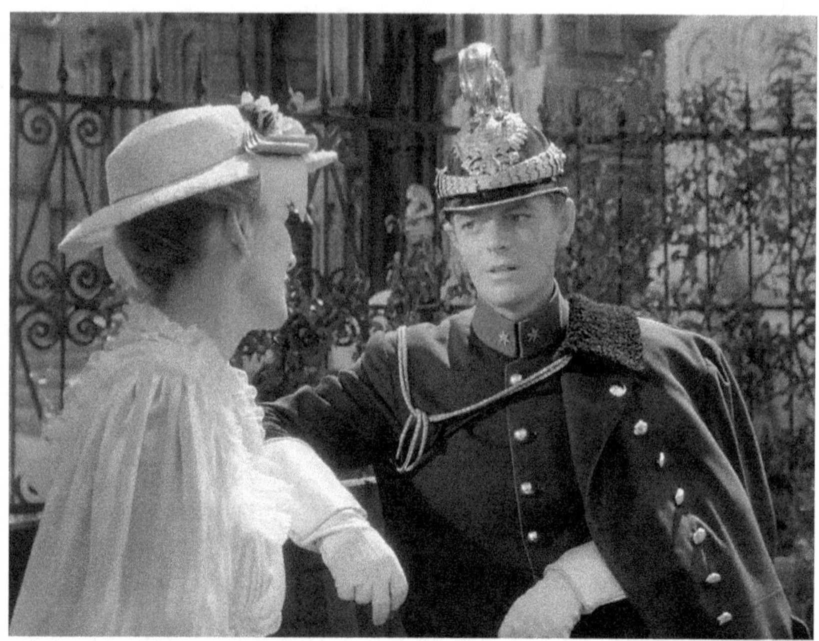

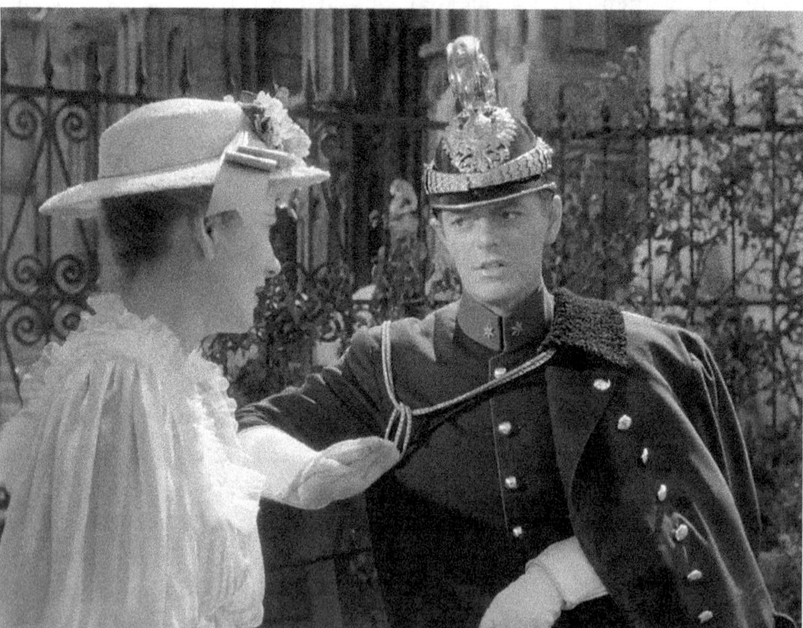

Figures 4.5 and 4.6. *Letter from an Unknown Woman*, dir. Max Ophuls, US, 1948. Digital frame grabs.

total cohesion? An assortment of behaviors, of actions and reactions; a nullity of setting and a maintenance of narrative. Prior discussion of the characters' thoughts and feelings turns into detailing of their behaviors.

These behaviors, moreover, are hardly unique. They are generic, habitual, and socially sanctioned. The figures on film simply carry them out and, in so doing, carry them on to others. They belong neither to her nor to him because, as behaviors, they do not belong to anyone. Their general structure precedes all who use them. To study them closely is thus to dissolve the fictional human figures into that structure. And the dissolution is literal as one starts and stops the filmstrip, breaking actions into gestures and words into phonemes. These details of behavior are disclosed by machinery; nullity of setting is the price paid for detail. One is then pushed past the concept of fiction as a stage for some figures in settings that express them. Under this concept, setting integrated characters. The critic was one who extolled that integration. One can hardly extoll anything else if and when one cannot see anything else. But criticism changes when performed at the level of character happenings of subsecond duration. It changes in accord with a change in its object, which now is segmented and repeatable indefinitely. It trades out its method for a new method, its concept for another still dimly perceived. For it is no longer the study of fiction or, at least, not only of fiction. It is natural history, the study of the organism: the study of what is called human behavior.

Coda

Indexical

In our reflections on the human figure we began with the image of a rough piece of stone—a stone we then proceed to cut and to polish until it has facets, as a gem cutter would. At the same time we allowed for a bit of wear around the edges so that we might see some overlap across its four sides. Perhaps a change of metaphor will not meet too much resistance at this late stage of our figural inquiry. That of the stone, while useful, is a trifle misleading. It implies that we can and do approach the human figure without any concept, as "a rough piece of stone." This seems to me doubtful. There may be a play of concepts—now this one, now that—but to come unequipped with any concept at all is rather unlikely for the mature and adult mind. The human figure may be more akin to a carpet whose corners each form one distinguishing concept: natural, pictorial, institutional, fictional. As we move closer to one of the corners, its concept grows in strength, but it remains on a continuum with the three others. We do not find four figures in the corners of the carpet, for the figure is the carpet, whole and entire. And it is difficult to lift one corner of the carpet without lifting at least one other for our reflection. This, in any case, is what our studies suggested.

What unites these four studies is an impulse toward continuity, in the sense of graduality or an absence of gaps. For each the human figure is ideally integrated into its ground, which varies with the concept. Here it is society, there, the picture plane; here the movie studio and there, the world of fiction.

We have seen that Ray Birdwhistell would not even consider a film of one person to be a useful record. His figure is always a living, social organism and is thereby involved in a social environment. This environment is really a matrix of communications that ensnare the human organism when still in the womb. Despite working in a clinic where he frequently encountered extremes of detachment, neurosis, and anxiety, Birdwhistell finds on film the continuity he seeks: the visible signs of social maintenance and integration. He does this by looking past the obvious picture that the film seems to show when played at normal speed; he goes deeper and deeper into the image until the figures start dancing at subsecond intervals. Here everything gives help to everything else, at the levels of the social and of the picture.

In the work of Victor Freeburg, the picture is all that matters. This picture must be beautiful, giving pleasure to eye and mind. Integration for Freeburg is a formal ideal, hence his figure is just a shape—a figure in the strong sense. And it must be handled gingerly so as not to make things ugly. It easily assumes its place in a harmonious composition but as soon as it starts moving, trouble arises. What feels good to the living organism is bad for the picture. Perhaps Freeburg errs in imposing his ideal of harmony on films of dramatic narrative, whose construction he was paid to teach. But he does seem to need the image of a living person to give dignity to the proceedings, which could otherwise be cartoons. He ends up by resenting and decrying the actor whose vanity is at odds with the needs of pictorial unity.

This is the figure that Hortense Powdermaker tries to seize: the actor engaged in a struggle for power. She sees the movie camera as an agent of power and its frame line as something like a rod of correction. She can hardly look at actors without feeling a twinge of sympathy for their various hardships, like their treatment as passive objects. She can hardly look without this feeling because she knows so much of how films are made, as reported to her in interviews—no matter how much the movies try to erase their own production. The erasure, in any case, is not quite complete because there the actors are in their splendor and misery. Paradoxically, while the dominant note here is conflict, the figure is bound even further by the image—is made continuous with the institution whose machinery is partly visible. This might tell us something about an actor's performance; then again, it might not.

It definitely tells us nothing about the world of fiction these actors are presumably helping to construct. This is what V. F. Perkins wants to show us. He apprehends the figure most immediately as a character; he praises the films where characters and settings are most related. This relation means more than just to be sited as a geometric point in coordinate space; more even than to be visible against a credible background that gives reality to the figure, although that is important too. It consists of a deeper tie between inner and outer, character and setting, so that both are imbued with a sense of significance. But it seems like such a synthesis is rather hard to accomplish at every moment of a film while still retaining credibility. In fact it seems rather rare, the exception and not the rule, even in fiction films that one would deem great. So if there is unity all the way down, one must find it hiding out—at the level of behavior.

We end up in a place much like where we began, revealing in hindsight that the starting point was arbitrary. But we had to start somewhere in order to move at all. Our movement has really been movement in a circle as we walked around the carpet, picking up its corners. As for the walk itself, it has occasionally been unsteady. Yet the concepts have worked to steady our step with their strong impulses toward continuity.

Other concepts could be chosen, and different connections drawn among those I did choose. The four examined here seemed sufficiently broad to include a wide range of analytic projects. Still, some would say I have neglected the most important concept, the one that essentially underpins the others. They might say I have ignored the force that is inherent in the preposition of this book's title. The human figure, yes—but the human figure *on film*. Such a phrase draws attention to the material support that presents the human figure for our inspection. After all, our historical materials have not been concerned with "the moving image," "time-based media," or some other generic category. Each of our writers was looking at films: films that were made on film, analog films. That analog has properties distinct from those of digital is entirely possible and at least worth considering. Its associated concept, the indexical figure, might have the strongest impulse to continuity of all.

In analog photography, a photograph is part of a photochemical process requiring light and real objects to which the film is present. The human figures it depicts are then also real objects to which the film was present at the time of exposure. And any copy of the film is still formed in direct descent from the original by means of light as well. Thus the photo is a form of what has been called the index. An indexical sign is one that allows us to infer the probable cause of the sign from the sign itself. The form of a footprint is the best known example: it points us to the foot whose impression it is. Likewise, the contents of a photograph point us to the objects whose presence and shape were needed to form the print before us. Analog film is a form of photography and shares, automatically, in its indexical process. Hence any human figure, whatever concept we apply, would also be indexical when we see it on strips of film.

I have spoken of film as an indexical process as if this had only material implications. Yet it is easily bound up with metaphysical notions, namely those about the world that is to be indexed. When Maurice Merleau-Ponty wrote, in 1947, that film is a tool of phenomenological philosophy, he meant that film and phenomenology share in the project of disclosing relations between self and world. While the philosopher could explain that there is no self without world—that the self is always outside itself in the surrounding world—the filmmaker showed such relation directly, simply by filming the self in its world. Emotions, for instance, are not private feelings; rather "they are types of behavior or styles of conduct which are visible from the outside."[1] And the medium of film records without fuss "the union of mind and body, mind and world."[2]

It seems unlikely that André Bazin could have failed to know this essay. For it appeared in the pages of *Les Temps Modernes* only several months after his "The Technique of *Citizen Kane*." In a sense, Bazin's extensive efforts in film criticism and theory were based on the logic of this phenomenology.[3] That there was some relation of person to environment, figure to ground, is an idea most explicit in his dislike of the close-up, "for it necessarily dissociates the actors from their surroundings." It gives the false impression that they exist in a world apart from "the wind in their hair, or the movement of a distant branch."[4] Bazin was unable to say exactly why this wind and this branch are important for us to see in addition to the figure. Nonetheless he was convinced that they absolutely are and thus merit inclusion in any film's mise-en-scène.

So the spatial and temporal unity of the image is the unity of the world that its frame can enclose: such is Bazin's explicit metaphysics. Hence the photograph is no mere image, it is a "fact," a piece of space and time cut out for all to see.[5] Even if filmmakers use their hands to push down the button to trigger the shutter to make the process start, it is the world itself that writes, that makes its own mark, by means of delicate ray-pencils emanating from the sun. The photographic image, from which the film is built, records the fact of its presence at particular sites and times. The light that hits the object is the light that hits the lens and unleashes the entire chemical process. Object, camera, film are touched by light. Whatever else the human figure on film might come to mean, it is the trace of an encounter preserved by means of light.

"This cultural understanding, however, has surely been changing for some time," wrote D. N. Rodowick in 2007. "In digital photography, the spatial link of physical causality is broken as well as the temporal continuity of the transformation."[6] That is to say, the luminous chain linking object to lens to photographic image has finally been cut. Light that passes through a digital camera is converted into series of binary numbers. The lens becomes the input of a computer that does not transcribe the object but transcodes it instead. It overlays a grid wherein each point of space is autonomous, discrete, and practically infinitely manipulable.[7] When this transcoded data is then converted back to image—perhaps no different perceptually from a photographic image—its being, says Rodowick, is inherently different. The action of the light has been interrupted and made to pass through this numerical detour. The image, the film, is no longer bound ontologically to its referent. Indeed, it does not need a referent in the sense of an external object. Such objects are now mere items of convenience when computer-generated imagery falls short of passable realism. And having been reduced to number and algorithm, ones and zeroes and zeroes and ones, the image is far more prone to further operations than the relatively nondiscrete image on film. Every point on its grid, that is every pixel, can be altered independently of the millions of others. Any blemish or error can be painted over, easily. The world does not write itself through digital cameras. Rather, it becomes the raw material for the user of an interface. In Rodowick's "Give me the instructions, and I will build you another image," one hears the distrust of that *mathesis universalis* once heralded by Descartes's "Give me matter and motion, and I shall make the world once more."[8]

These comments apply to the digital image tout court. Let us see how they pertain to the human figure specifically. In digital cinema, this figure is also transcoded numerically as light hits the body and passes through the lens. It is then on equal terms with everything else that has been transcoded, including synthesized materials without physical referents. The figure is also equally manipulable, meaning in this case practically infinitely manipulable. On celluloid film, its transformations were limited primarily to two discrete stages in the filmmaking process: operations on the figure prior to filming, in terms of cosmetics, and after filming was completed, in the editing of sequences. One could change the background that appears behind the figure, a process known as rear projection; one could also bring figures from separate shots or takes together through the technique of matte work, a forebear of compositing. Still, one was stuck with the basic indexical figure, which more or less resisted the artist's designs. No matter how much the figure was covered with makeup, or its bits of performance rearranged by editing, or its backgrounds and companions added in postproduction—each image of the figure preserved the existence and concrete duration of a once-living being. Such would be lost or seriously impaired when the inner contents of an image are cleverly altered, and with a digital image one can never be sure just how much or how little is already altered. One could even say with Rodowick that it "wants" to be altered.[9]

This trend toward unreality reaches its limit with the widespread phenomenon of motion capture performance. The indexical and the coded are united not just in a single film image but in a single human figure. Motion capture is a process where the body of the actor is made discrete and digital prior to filming. The actor will put on a formfitting suit, frequently black, that is covered with small reflective circles called markers. These markers are placed at important points of structure like joints and limb endings and the muscles of the face. Then the actor is filmed by a battery of cameras—a few dozen for the body and even more for the face—which record the reflections coming off the markers. These luminous data are fed into a computer to make a three-dimensional model, a cloud of moving points. And as the actor moves around, the "marker cloud" shifts; it remains without contour until mapped onto a "puppet." The cameras, and through them the computer, do not record the whole figure that now stands before them. They capture only points of discrete articulation off which the light reflects into the camera lenses. The rest is filtered out. That includes skin and hair. Filming takes place against a green or black background, and the actors with whom one eventually shares a scene are probably not present to deliver their lines. The graphics technicians will work up this material that consists of pure kinesis sampled from figures. The kinetic cloud or puppet can then be fleshed out. Usually, it becomes something quite fantastical, a monster or an animal with intelligence and speech. The motion capture process is used in video games as well, which proves how far film is no longer film.

The resulting figure is a paradoxical thing. It is, on the one hand, the trace of real movements that one would not need if one could make them from scratch. Designers evidently still have trouble producing figures that move and act convincingly without this human input. On the other hand this input is no less subject than any other to the terms of practically infinite manipulability. Indeed the verb *capture* suggests that such motion has been stolen from its owner and turned to ends unforeseen. The original motion can be tweaked to high heaven and it is impossible to know who or what moves the figure. All of this follows from Rodowick's argument and has been developed in recent literature on motion capture.[10]

Such advances in imaging occasion reflection. The moving image has changed, is changing, and so creates an epistemological crisis for those who thought they knew film. There are two main responses to this situation. The first is to affirm the radical difference between analog and digital, and so to see the former in sharper relief. The second is to seek out hidden resemblances, thus blurring the boundaries of analog and digital.

~

With regard to the human figure, we can explore this second option by means of some examples drawn from Method acting; for the Method is often thought of as a technique for the manifestation of presence onscreen. And when motion capture actors deny any difference between motion capture and traditional forms of acting—using a Method language of emotion and conviction—they are doubted by scholars, who find these invocations both corny and false. For how could inner feeling be bodied forth by a marker cloud, mapped onto a puppet, overlaid with tentacles or the paw pads of an ape? Since the Method is certainly the most influential form of training for actors since World War II, let us look at how it works to manifest presence, which has implications for continuity as well. We could hardly do worse than begin with its founder, the teacher Lee Strasberg and his book *A Dream of Passion*.

The actor's first task, he tells us, is the reduction of tension both physical and mental. This requires the flexing and relaxing of each skeletal muscle, one at a time, as well as standard vocal exercise. Relaxation is preliminary to the work of concentration, and "concentration is the key to what has been loosely thought of as imagination."[11] Concentration begins with objects, for instance, a cup of coffee. The actor aims attention at a real cup of coffee; at its texture, shape, color, and weight; at the heat of the liquid felt through its container. Then the focus shifts to the liquid itself: its color, taste, texture, aroma, the sound that it makes when sloshed around gently. Concentrating on the object, the actor dissects it, one sense at a time. "Then the actor performs the exercise without the presence of the object."[12] This process is repeated with many other objects until the actor is quite comfortable in a world of imaginary objects, to which she or he responds as if they were real. Such work is premised on the notion of affective memory, or the ability to feel past feelings by evoking their original objects. A similar exercise requires the actor to go through the motions of grooming or hygiene, without any razor, hairbrush, and so on. In another, one sits in a chair and produces the warmth of an imaginary sunshine hitting one's skin. In another, one tries to feel naked while still fully clothed. All of this is meant to disinhibit the actor's instrument so that she or he may turn it to imaginative ends.

Of course, the most famous part of the American Method is the so-called emotional-memory exercise. Now the actor tries to substitute her or his past experience for the experience of the character as the author has written it. Strasberg relates one particular such exercise that begins with a woman saying, "It's cold"—coldness, for her, being the strongest aspect of a prior experience once fraught with emotion.

> We then go on to see if the actress is locating that sensation in different parts of the body—the hairline, etc. The actress then says that she feels a certain kind of cold in certain places.
>
> "Well," I say to her, "take each place separately and try to see if you can remember the kind of cold that existed there. And see if, with the memory, you will be able to recapture some of that cold. And don't worry if it doesn't happen; just make the effort. Don't worry if you cannot swim. You simply keep moving your arms; you won't drown."
>
> As the exercise proceeds, I ask the actress to remember what she was wearing, the material, etc., in an effort to recreate more details. The actress remembers that the material felt cold on her hands.
>
> The exercise then continues as the actress recreates more of the details: the crinkly sound of the ground; later a dusty smell in the air; still later a voice, "shallow, like an echo." As the sound of the voice becomes stronger for the actress, she begins to sob.
>
> "Wait a minute! Wait a minute, wait a minute!" she wails as the emotion breaks through.
>
> In recreating the details of the original emotional memory, the actress recreated the original emotion.[13]

Half of the Method, then, is a derealization of really existing objects so one can move in a world of fantasy. The other half consists in diving deep into one's past to revivify experiences unrelated to the present. This is the source of the apparent authenticity that would be lost in the synthetic actor's non-presence. And this is the practice that has shaped actor training of almost all kinds for over half a century.[14]

I remind the reader of such procedures in the training of actors because they trouble easy notions of presence and continuity. An actor who revives a sensation of coldness—and, with that, an emotional experience—is a figure who is both indexically present and existentially not present at the same time. The actor withdraws utterly from the physical surround. Moreover, such withdrawal is always possible in less extreme forms: in distraction, inattention, the state of being "not all there." Yet the ontology of film and its concept of the index are premised precisely on being-all-there; indeed, one would not lament the transcoding and compositing if one did not ascribe this quality to the world that is sourced. That is why our example of the Method gives pause: in its quest for real emotion, it becomes an art of not relating to the present situation. And when it does relate to the present situation, it transforms the surrounding objects into something else—something imaginary, something as-if, something that is there and yet also is not.

This form of non-relation is but another variant of other such forms we have explored in this study. The naturalist, the pictorialist, the institutionalist, and the critic of fiction each sought from film a kind of continuity—of an organism with its environment, of a shape with its picture, of an actor with the studio, of a character with the setting. Respectively, they ignored or decried the indifference of the organism to its environment; the discord of the shape brought on by its movement; the ability of the actor to really play characters; the necessity for characters to fall out of phase with settings. That the human figure might not be present, might be aloof or absent, somehow withdrawing from the entwinement of all with all: this would be a source of major embarrassment. One could acknowledge it in theory but disregard it in practice in favor of that which displays continuity. It may be the case, as Georg Henrik von Wright suggests, that the idea of continuity has a palliative function, "smoothing the rough surface" of the world as we find it.[15] The human figure on film is one source of this roughness and, naturally, we have our ways of smoothing it.

But since the digital prompts our reassessment of film, we reassess also the status of its human figure. The ontologist might say that this figure is present and continuous with its surroundings if we see them on film. I have tried instead to show just how often this figure is neither present at the time of filming nor continuous with its surroundings. Consequently, it would be neither present nor continuous with its surroundings when we see it move before us on some strips of film. Perhaps we do not mind, since we usually keep on looking.

Notes

Introduction

1. D. H. Lawrence, *Sons and Lovers* (1913; repr., New York: Viking, 1958), 298.

2. Stephen Heath, *Questions of Cinema* (Bloomington: Indiana University Press, 1981), 12.

3. Frank Norris, *McTeague: A Story of San Francisco* (New York: Oxford University Press, 1995), 86.

4. Howard Hawks, quoted in Joseph McBride, *Hawks on Hawks* (Lexington: University Press of Kentucky, 2013), 129.

5. Robert Sklar, *City Boys: Cagney, Bogart, Garfield* (Princeton, NJ: Princeton University Press, 1992), 172.

6. A. M. Sperber and Eric Lax, *Bogart* (New York: William Morrow and Co., 1997), 269.

7. R. G. Collingwood, *An Essay on Philosophical Method* (1933; repr., Oxford: Oxford University Press, 2005), 50.

8. Stanley Cavell, *The World Viewed: Reflections on the Ontology of Cinema*, enlarged ed. (Cambridge, MA: Harvard, 1979), 26; italics in original.

9. Ford Madox Ford, *The Good Soldier: A Tale of Passion* (1915; repr., New York: Penguin, 1946), 113.

10. Steven Shaviro, *The Cinematic Body* (Minneapolis: University of Minnesota Press, 1993), 23.

11. Shaviro, *The Cinematic Body*, 32.

12. Shaviro, 255–58.

13. See, for example, Linda Williams, "Film Bodies: Gender, Genre, and Excess," *Film Quarterly* 44, no. 4 (1991): 2–13; Vivian Sobchack, *The Address of the Eye: A Phenomenology of Film Experience* (Princeton, NJ: Princeton University Press, 1990), 164–259; Laura U. Marks, *The Skin of the Film: Intercultural Cinema, Embodiment, and the Senses* (Durham, NC: Duke University Press,

2000); and Jennifer M. Barker, *The Tactile Eye: Touch and the Cinematic Experience* (Berkeley: University of California Press, 2009). There is also an older trope of film as hysterical body: see Thomas Elsaesser, "Tales of Sound and Fury: Observations on the Family Melodrama," *Monogram*, no. 4 (1972): 2–15.

14. Shaviro, *The Cinematic Body*, 259–60.

15. Shaviro, 112.

16. Shaviro, 108.

17. Shaviro, 121.

18. Shaviro, 116.

19. Shaviro, 111.

20. Elias Canetti, *The Torch in My Ear* (1980), trans. Joachim Neugroschel, in *The Memoirs of Elias Canetti* (New York: Farrar, Straus, and Giroux, 1999), 545.

21. Canetti, 546.

Chapter 1

1. Émile Gaboriau, *Monsieur Lecoq*, trans. Laura E. Kendall (1869; repr., New York: Dover, 1975), 180–81.

2. Marston Bates, *The Nature of Natural History*, rev. ed. (New York: Scribner, 1961), 7.

3. Ray L. Birdwhistell, *Kinesics and Context: Essays on Body Motion Communication* (Philadelphia: University of Pennsylvania Press, 1970), 12.

4. Ray McDermott, "Profile: Ray L. Birdwhistell," *Kinesis Report* 2, no. 3 (1980): 14.

5. For general biography, see Adam Kendon and Stuart J. Sigman, "Commemorative Essay: Ray L. Birdwhistell (1918–1994)," *Semiotica* 112, nos. 3–4 (1996): 231–61; Wendy Leeds-Hurwitz, "Notes in the History of Intercultural Communication: The Foreign Service Institute and the Mandate for Intercultural Training," *Quarterly Journal of Speech* 76, no. 3 (1990): 262–81; Martha Davis, "Film Projectors as Microscopes: Ray L. Birdwhistell and Microanalysis of Interaction (1955–1975)," *Visual Anthropology Review* 17, no. 2 (2001–2002): 39–49.

6. Al Capp, *Li'l Abner: The Frazetta Years, Vol. 1, 1954–1955*, ed. Denis Kitchen (Milwaukie, OR: Dark Horse Press, 2003), 83–85.

7. Paul Byers, "A Personal View of Nonverbal Communication," *Theory into Practice* 16, no. 3 (1977): 135.

8. See Ray L. Birdwhistell, *Introduction to Kinesics: An Annotation System for Analysis of Body Motion and Gesture* (Washington, DC: U.S. Department of State, Foreign Service Institute, 1952); Birdwhistell, "Kinesics," in *The*

Body Reader: Social Aspects of the Human Body, ed. Ted Polhemus (New York: Pantheon, 1978), 284–94; Wendy Leeds Hurwitz and Stuart J. Sigman, "The Penn Tradition," in *The Social History of Language and Social Interaction Research: People, Places, Ideas*, ed. Wendy Leeds-Hurwitz (Cresskill, NJ: Hampton Press, 2010), 235–70.

9. Ray L. Birdwhistell, "The Language of the Body: The Natural Environment of Words," in *Human Communication: Theoretical Explorations*, ed. Albert Silverstein (Hillsdale, NJ: Lawrence Erlbaum, 1974), 215.

10. Ray L. Birdwhistell, "Lecture at American Museum of Natural History, October 4, 1980," in *Holisms of Communication: The Early History of Audio-Visual Sequence Analysis*, eds. James McElvenny and Andrea Ploder (Berlin: Language Science Press, 2021), 254.

11. Ray Birdwhistell, "Training in Cultural Observation," *Human Organization Clearing-House Bulletin* 3, no. 3 (1955): 31.

12. I have not successfully found a complete print of *Sports Day*, a J. Arthur Rank production directed by Francis Searle. However, a shorter version was released as *Colonel's Cup* the same year, apparently recut to emphasize the rising star Jean Simmons (misspelled "Simmonds" here). *Colonel's Cup* exists as a Gaumont-British International 16mm "Moviepak" edition for home viewing, and this is the version of the film I have consulted.

13. Birdwhistell, "Lecture at American Museum of Natural History," 253.

14. Compare Karl G. Heider, *Ethnographic Film*, 2nd ed. (Austin: University of Texas Press, 2006), 114: "whole bodies, whole interactions, and whole people in whole acts."

15. Ben Brewster and Leah Jacobs, *Theatre to Cinema* (New York: Oxford University Press, 1997), 33–78.

16. Birdwhistell, *Kinesics and Context*, 12.

17. This film is called *A Context Analysis of Family Interviews* (1974); the narrators are Christian Beels and Jane Ferber.

18. See Ray L. Birdwhistell, "The Use of Audio-Visual Teaching Aids," in *Resources for the Teaching of Anthropology*, eds. David G. Mandelbaum, Gabriel W. Lasker, and Ethel M. Albert (Berkeley: University of California Press, 1963), 49–61; Birdwhistell, *Kinesics and Context*, 147–55; Adam Kendon, "Some Theoretical and Methodological Aspects of the Use of Film in the Study of Social Interaction," in *Emerging Strategies in Social Psychological Research*, ed. G. P. Ginsburg (London: Wiley, 1979), 67–91; Albert E. Scheflen, "Natural History Method in Psychotherapy: Communicational Research," in *Methods of Research in Psychotherapy*, eds. Louis A. Gottschalk and Arthur H. Auerbach (New York: Appleton-Century-Crofts, 1966), 263–89; Albert E. Scheflen, *Communicational Structure: Analysis of a Psychotherapy Transaction* (Bloomington: Indiana University Press, 1973), 311–39; Jacques Van Vlack, "The Research

Document Film," *American Science Film Association Notes* 1, no. 5 (1965): 9–11; and Jacques Van Vlack, "Filming Psychotherapy from the Viewpoint of a Research Cinematographer," in *Methods of Research in Psychotherapy*, 13–24.

19. Scheflen, *Communicational Structure*, 319.

20. Birdwhistell, *Kinesics and Context*, 22–23.

21. Birdwhistell, 23.

22. I borrow the term from Katie Joice, "Mothering in the Frame: Cinematic Microanalysis and the Pathogenic Mother, 1945–1967," *History of the Human Sciences* 34, no. 5 (2021): 105–31.

23. Deborah Weinstein, *The Pathological Family: Postwar America and the Rise of Family Therapy* (Ithaca, NY: Cornell University Press, 2013), 31ff.

24. Gregory Bateson, "Communication," in *The Natural History of an Interview*, ed. Norman McQuown (Chicago: University of Chicago Library, Department of Photoduplication, 1971), chap. 1, p. 12; italics removed.

25. See Wendy Leeds-Hurwitz and Adam Kendon, "*The Natural History of an Interview* and the Microanalysis of Behavior in Social Interaction: A Critical Moment in Research Practice," in *Holisms of Communication*, 145–200.

26. See Henning Engelke, "Perception, Awareness, and Film Practice: A Natural History of the 'Doris Film,' " in *Holisms of Communication*, 103–35.

27. Quoted in Bernard Dionysius Geoghegan, "The Family as Machine: Film, Infrastructure, and Cybernetic Kinship in Suburban America," *Grey Room*, no. 66 (2017): 87.

28. Gregory Bateson, "The Actors and the Setting," in *The Natural History of an Interview*, chap. 5, p. 1.

29. Ray L. Birdwhistell, "Dinner Address, Eastern Modern Language Association," 1 April 1966, in box 16, Ray L. Birdwhistell Papers, Folklore Archives, Penn Museum.

30. Birdwhistell in Norman A. McQuown, "Collation," in *The Natural History of an Interview*, chap. 9, p. 6.

31. Ray L. Birdwhistell, "Crowd Scene," n.d. (ca. 1956–1959), box 16, Birdwhistell Papers.

32. Birdwhistell, *Kinesics and Context*, 245.

33. Birdwhistell, 228–29.

34. Birdwhistell, 245.

Chapter 2

1. C. K. Ogden and I. A. Richards, *The Meaning of Meaning* (1923; repr., San Diego: Harcourt Brace Jovanovich, 1989), 139–59.

2. Zeynep Çelik Alexander, *Kinaesthetic Knowing: Aesthetics, Epistemology, Modern Design* (Chicago: University of Chicago Press, 2017), 1–26, 167–201.

3. Roger Fry, *Vision and Design* (London: Chatto and Windus, 1920), 23.

4. Virginia Woolf, *Roger Fry* (1940; repr., New York: Mariner, 1976), 247.

5. Hans Richter, "The Badly Trained Sensibility" (1924), trans. Mike Weaver, in *The Avant-Garde Film: A Reader of Theory and Criticism*, ed. P. Adams Sitney (New York: Anthology Film Archives, 1987), 22–23.

6. Biographical data comes from "Mr. Freeburg Receives Ph.D. From Columbia University," *Haverford News* 7, no. 8 (April 13, 1915): 1; "Freeburg, Victor Oscar," in *Who Was Who in American History: Arts and Letters* (Chicago: Marquis Who's Who, 1975), 170; and a two-page curriculum vitae ca. 1921, box 2, folder 16, Victor Oscar Freeburg Papers, Sterling Memorial Library, Yale University.

7. The book is Frances Taylor Patterson, *Cinema Craftsmanship* (New York: Harcourt, Brace, 1920); see "Prof. Freeburg Sues for Share in Book," *Variety*, April 22, 1921, 46.

8. Victor Oscar Freeburg, *Disguise Plots in Elizabethan Drama: A Study in Stage Tradition* (New York: Columbia University Press, 1915), 60.

9. Freeburg, *The Art of Photoplay Making*, 28.

10. Freeburg, 36.

11. Victor Oscar Freeburg, *Pictorial Beauty on the Screen* (New York: Macmillan, 1923), 94.

12. Freeburg, *The Art of Photoplay Making*, 64.

13. Victor Oscar Freeburg, "At My Window," *Los Angeles Herald*, November 16, 1909.

14. Primary sources for Photoplay Composition at Columbia include "True Purposes of Columbia's Course in 'Movie' Play Writing," *New York Sun*, October 17, 1915; "Lasky Company Offers Scholarship to Columbia Students," *Moving Picture World* 26, no. 5 (October 30, 1915): 765; Arthur Leeds, "Thinks and Things," *Writer's Monthly* 7, no. 1 (January, 1916): 31; Epes Winthrop Sargent, "Wanted—A Museum," *Moving Picture World* 29, no. 11 (September 9, 1916): 1704; "October 16 is Date Set By Lasky For Its Prize Play," *Motion Picture News* 14, no. 16 (October 21, 1916): 2551; B. F. Barrett, "The Photoplay Scenario: An Interview With Prof. Freeburg," *Motography* 16, no. 20 (November 11, 1916): 1077–78; "The Drews at Columbia," *Moving Picture World* 30, no. 13 (December 30, 1916): 1945; "Home-Made Motion Pictures Predicted for Near Future," *New York Times*, April 22, 1917; "Flashes From the World of Cinema," *New York Sun*, July 15, 1917; "Taking the Movies to College at Columbia University," *New York Tribune*, August 10, 1919; and annual editions from 1915 to 1919 of the *Columbia University Bulletin of Information: Extension Teaching Announcement* and *Summer Session Announcement*, Columbia University Archives. See also Dana Polan, *Scenes of Instruction: The Beginnings of the U.S. Study of Film* (Berkeley: University of California Press, 2007), 33–89; Peter Decherney, *Hollywood and the Cultural*

Elite: How the Movies Became American (New York: Columbia University Press, 2006), 41–62; Kaveh Askari, *Making Movies into Art: Picture Craft From the Magic Lantern to Early Hollywood* (London: BFI-Palgrave, 2014), 71–92.

15. Freeburg, *Pictorial Beauty on the Screen*, 106.

16. One might expect to find some discussion in Hugo Münsterberg's *The Photoplay*, given Münsterberg's other writing, but the subject is avoided, as if simply not relevant.

17. Vachel Lindsay, *The Art of the Moving Picture* (1915, rev. 1922; New York: Modern Library, 2000), 28, 124.

18. Lindsay, *The Art of the Moving Picture*, 80.

19. Vachel Lindsay to Louis and Jean Starr Untermeyer, February 27, 1917, in *Letters of Vachel Lindsay*, ed. Marc Chénetier (New York: Burt Franklin and Co., 1979), 143; also Lindsay, *The Art of the Moving Picture*, 6, 22.

20. Vernon Lee, *The Beautiful: An Introduction to Psychological Aesthetics* (Cambridge: Cambridge University Press, 1913), 53; quoted in Freeburg, *The Art of Photoplay Making*, 28. Compare Vernon Lee and C. Anstruther Thomson, "Beauty and Ugliness," in Vernon Lee, *Beauty and Ugliness and Other Studies in Psychological Aesthetics* (London: John Lane, 1912), 153–239.

21. Lord Shaftesbury, *Characteristicks of Men, Manners, Opinions, Times* (1711; repr., Indianapolis, IN: Liberty Fund, 2001), 2:193–94; Friedrich Schiller, *On the Aesthetic Education of Man in a Series of Letters*, trans. Reginald Snell (1795; repr., New Haven, CT: Yale University Press, 1954), 81; Immanuel Kant, *Critique of the Power of Judgment*, trans. Paul Guyer and Eric Matthews (1790; repr., New York: Cambridge University Press, 2001), 114.

22. Lee, *The Beautiful*, 13.

23. Richard Koszarski, *An Evening's Entertainment: The Age of the Silent Feature Picture, 1915–1928* (New York: Charles Scribner's Sons, 1990), 34–36, 56–61.

24. Freeburg, *Pictorial Beauty on the Screen*, 32.

25. Freeburg, 75–77.

26. Victor O. Freeburg, quoted in Barrett, "Photoplay Scenario," 1077.

27. Freeburg, *Pictorial Beauty on the Screen*, 36.

28. Freeburg, *The Art of Photoplay Making*, 31.

29. Freeburg, 71.

30. Freeburg, *Pictorial Beauty on the Screen*, 19.

31. Freeburg, 47.

32. A manuscript for *Pictorial Beauty on the Screen* was complete as early as 1921: Victor Oscar Freeburg, "[Diary: 'A Voyage of Poetic Adventure'],' entry for October 25, 1921, box 2, folder 16, Freeburg Papers.

33. Freeburg, *Pictorial Beauty on the Screen*, v.

34. Victor Oscar Freeburg, "Making America More American," *Swedish American Trade Journal* 15, no. 9 (1921): 332–34, and "'El Dorado' Rediscov-

ered," *Forum* 73, no. 4 (1925): 474–89. See also Gunlög Fur, *Painting Culture, Painting Nature: Stephen Mopope, Oscar Jacobson, and the Development of Indian Art in Oklahoma* (Norman: University of Oklahoma Press, 2019), 71–79.

35. Freeburg, *Pictorial Beauty on the Screen*, 9.

36. Freeburg, 9–10.

37. Freeburg, 133.

38. Freeburg, *The Art of Photoplay Making*, 95–96.

39. Freeburg, *Pictorial Beauty on the Screen*, 140.

40. Freeburg, 160.

41. Freeburg, 114.

42. Freeburg, 12.

43. Freeburg, 37.

44. Freeburg, 4.

45. Freeburg, 136.

46. Richard deCordova, *Picture Personalities: The Emergence of the Star System in America* (Urbana: University of Illinois Press, 2001), 106–7.

47. Freeburg, *The Art of Photoplay Making*, 78, 267, 10.

48. Freeburg, 59.

49. Victor Oscar Freeburg, letter to J. Hall Pleasants, September 18, 1949, box 1, folder 2, Freeburg Papers.

Chapter 3

1. Raymond Williams, *Keywords: A Vocabulary of Culture and Society*, rev. ed. (London: Fontana, 1988), 168–69. Emphasis in original.

2. Bronisław Malinowski, "Culture," in *Encyclopaedia of the Social Sciences* (New York: Macmillan, 1949), 4:626; see also Walton H. Hamilton, "Institutions," in *Encyclopaedia of the Social Sciences*, 8:84–89.

3. Hortense Powdermaker, "An Anthropologist Looks at the Movies," *Annals of the American Academy of Political and Social Science*, no. 254 (1947): 80. Compare Bronisław Malinowski, *A Scientific Theory of Culture and Other Essays* (Chapel Hill: University of North Carolina Press, 1944), 52–53.

4. Hortense Powdermaker, *Hollywood, the Dream Factory: An Anthropologist Looks at the Movie-makers* (Boston: Little, Brown, and Co., 1950), 207.

5. Hortense Powdermaker, quoted in "Life in Hollywood," *New Yorker*, March 5, 1949.

6. This account is based on material in the folder "Gr. #75, Powdermaker, Dr. Hortense, Queens College—Study of Motion Pictures as Part of United States Culture," box #MF-35, Wenner-Gren Foundation for Anthropological Research Files, New York; and Hortense Powdermaker, *Stranger and Friend: The Way of an Anthropologist* (New York: Norton, 1966),

209–31; see also Eric R. Wolf, "Hortense Powdermaker 1900–1970," *American Anthropologist* 73, no. 3 (1971): 783–86.

7. Richard Koszarski, "'It's No Use to Have an Unhappy Man': Paul Fejos at Universal," *Film History* 17, nos. 2/3 (2005): 234–40.

8. Powdermaker, *Stranger and Friend*, 210.

9. Hortense Powdermaker, "Review of *Movies: A Psychological Study* by Martha Wolfenstein and Nathan Leites," *Psychiatry* 14, no. 3 (1951): 353–55.

10. "Life in Hollywood," 25; Powdermaker to Fejos, June 4, 1947, in "Gr. #75, Powdermaker"; "Prof's Next Pic Tome," *Variety*, December 20, 1950. Powdermaker's last renewal petition to the Viking Fund was made on February 9, 1950, was declined on November 28 and formally withdrawn on December 5.

11. For example Terry Ramsaye, "An Anthropologist Looks at Hollywood," *Motion Picture Herald* 181, no. 2 (October 14, 1950), 21, 24; Herb Golden, "Hollywood as 'Dream Factory' Just Nightmare to Femme Anthropologist," *Variety*, October 18, 1950, 4, 18; Budd Schulberg, "Hollywood Primitive," *New York Times*, October 15, 1950; Arthur M. Schlesinger, Jr., "The Anthropological Fallacy," *The Nation*, December 30, 1950; Robert Bierstedt, "Review: *Hollywood, the Dream Factory*," *American Sociological Review* 16, no. 1 (1951): 124–25.

12. Hortense Powdermaker to Paul Fejos, August 4, 1946, in "Gr. #75, Powdermaker," Wenner-Gren Files.

13. Powdermaker, *Hollywood, the Dream Factory*, 185–87.

14. Powdermaker, 192.

15. Powdermaker, 254.

16. Powdermaker, 248.

17. Powdermaker, 220.

18. Powdermaker, "An Anthropologist Looks at the Movies, 87.

19. Powdermaker, *Hollywood, the Dream Factory*, 75.

20. Powdermaker, 76–77.

21. Powdermaker, 327.

22. Compare Danae Clark, in a book much influenced by Powdermaker: "[S]ocial relations have been embedded in the textual terrain of the film," but only because films "represent," "signify," or offer "discourse" or "commentary" on social relations. Clarke, *Negotiating Hollywood: The Cultural Politics of Actors' Labor* (Minneapolis: University of Minnesota, 1995), 83, 101, 91, 93.

23. Powdermaker, *Hollywood, the Dream Factory*, 224.

24. Hortense Powdermaker, *Life in Lesu: The Study of a Melanesian Society in New Ireland* (1933; repr., New York: Norton, 1971), 103–39.

25. Adrienne L. McLean, "Feeling and the Filmed Body: Judy Garland and the Kinesics of Suffering," *Film Quarterly* 55, no. 3 (2002): 2–15. See also Janet Staiger, *Interpreting Films: Studies in the Historical Reception of American Cinema* (Princeton, NJ: Princeton University Press, 1992), 154–77.

26. Powdermaker, *Hollywood, the Dream Factory*, 254.

27. Jeanine Basinger, *The Star Machine* (New York: Vintage, 2009), 188.

28. Lana Turner, *Lana: The Lady, the Legend, the Truth* (New York: E. P. Dutton, 1982), 25. Other sources for Turner's biography are Lou Valentino, *The Films of Lana Turner* (Secaucus, NJ: Citadel Press, 1976); and various articles in "Lana Turner Scrapbooks, 1939–1956," microfilm, Performing Arts Library, New York.

29. Compare Richard Dyer, "Four Films of Lana Turner," in *Star Texts: Image and Performance in Film and Television*, ed. Jeremy G. Butler (Detroit, MI: Wayne State University Press, 1991), 214–27.

30. Turner, *Lana*, 178.

31. Turner, 136.

32. Turner, 137–39.

33. Vincente Minnelli (as told to Hector Arce), *I Remember it Well* (London: Angus and Robertson, 1975), 254.

34. John Houseman, *Front and Center* (New York: Simon and Schuster, 1979), 375.

35. Powdermaker, *Stranger and Friend*, 13.

36. Powdermaker, 222.

37. Lillian Ross, "Picture" (1952), in *Reporting* (New York: Dodd, Mead, and Co., 1981), 301.

38. Powdermaker, *Stranger and Friend*, 230.

39. Powdermaker, 286.

Chapter 4

1. Catherine Gallagher, "The Rise of Fictionality," in *The Novel, Volume 1: History, Geography, and Culture*, ed. Franco Moretti (Princeton, NJ: Princeton University Press, 2006), 336–63.

2. Ian Watt, *The Rise of the Novel* (1957; repr., Berkeley: University of California Press, 2001), 26.

3. Bliss Perry, *A Study of Prose Fiction*, rev. ed. (Boston: Houghton Mifflin, 1920); also Clayton Hamilton, *The Art of Fiction: A Formulation of Its Fundamental Principles* (New York: Odyssey Press, 1939).

4. Yuri Tsivian, "Some Historical Footnotes to the Kuleshov Experiment," trans. Kathy Porter, in *Early Cinema: Space, Frame, Narrative*, ed. Thomas Elsaesser (London: BFI, 1990), 249–50.

5. Mark Shivas, "Minnelli's Method," *Movie*, no. 1 (1962): 17–19; Robin Wood, "Attitudes in *Advise and Consent*," *Movie*, no. 4 (1962): 14–17; unsigned, "Howard Hawks," *Movie*, no. 5 (1962): 7; unsigned [Ian A. Cameron], "Against *This Sporting Life*," *Movie*, no. 10 (1963): 21–22; V. F. Perkins, "*King of Kings*," *Movie*, no. 1 (1962): 29–30; Mark Shivas, "New Approach," *Movie*, no. 8 (1963): 13–15.

6. Details on *Movie*'s beginnings can be found in John Gibbs, *The Life of Mise-en-Scène: Visual Style and British Film Criticism, 1946–1978* (Manchester, UK: Manchester University Press, 2013), 95–193; also Jeffrey Crouse, "Fueled by Enthusiasms: Jeffrey Crouse Interviews V. F. Perkins," *Film International* 2, no. 3 (2004): 17–19.

7. V. F. Perkins, "The British Cinema," *Movie*, no. 1 (1962): 5.

8. Fereydoun Hoveyda, "Nicholas Ray's Reply: Party Girl" (from *Cahiers du Cinéma*, 107, May 1960), trans. Norman King, in *Cahiers du Cinéma: 1960s: New Wave, New Cinema, Reevaluating Hollywood*, ed. Jim Hillier (Cambridge, MA: Harvard University Press, 1986), 123.

9. V. F. Perkins, "Nicholas Ray," *Oxford Opinion*, no. 40 (1960): 31–33.

10. Henry James, *The Portrait of a Lady* (1881; repr., New York: P. F. Collier and Son, 1917), 600.

11. V. F. Perkins, *Film as Film: Understanding and Judging Movies* (Harmondsworth, UK: Penguin, 1972), 69. He revisits the subject in "Where is the World? The Horizon of Events in Movie Fiction," in *Style and Meaning: Studies in the Detailed Analysis of Film*, ed. John Gibbs and Douglas Pye (Manchester, UK: Manchester University Press, 2005), 16–41.

12. V. F. Perkins, "A Reply to Sam Rohdie," *Screen* 13, no. 4 (1972): 149.

13. Perkins, *Film as Film*, 25.

14. V. F. Perkins, "Charm and Blood," *Oxford Opinion*, no. 42 (1960): 34.

15. Adrian Martin, "Available to Enjoyment (and Not Just in a Hedonistic Way): An Appreciation of Victor Perkins," Warwick Film and Television Studies, https://warwick.ac.uk/fac/arts/film/archive/vfp/adrianmartin.

16. I borrow this figure from David Bordwell, *Making Meaning: Inference and Rhetoric in the Interpretation of Cinema* (Cambridge, MA: Harvard University Press, 1989), 170–81. See also Adrian Martin, *Mise en Scène and Film Style: From Classical Hollywood to New Media Art* (London: Palgrave Macmillan, 2014), 22–24.

17. Ian Cameron et al., "Method: Vincente Minnelli," *Movie*, no. 1 (1962): 21–24.

18. Perkins, *Film as Film*, 76. Compare Barry Boys, "*The Courtship of Eddie's Father*," *Movie*, no. 10 (1963): 29–32; the similarity suggests that Perkins may have read it in lieu of rewatching the film itself.

19. V. F. Perkins in Ian Cameron et al., "*Movie* Differences," *Movie*, no. 8 (1963): 28. Compare V. F. Perkins, "*Vivre sa Vie*," in *The Films of Jean-Luc Godard*, ed. Ian Cameron (New York: Praeger, 1969), 32–39.

20. Charles Barr, "Dolce Vita," *Granta* 64, no. 1207 (1961): 20.

21. Charles Barr, "*The Entertainer*," *Granta* 64, no. 1202 (1960): 33.

22. Charles Barr, "CinemaScope: Before and After," *Film Quarterly* 16, no. 4 (1963): 20.

23. Barr, "CinemaScope," 22.

24. Barr, 23.

25. Barr, 14.

26. Thomas Hardy, quoted in Barr, "CinemaScope," 15.

27. Barr, "CinemaScope," 16.

28. Robert Liddell, *Robert Liddell on the Novel* (Chicago: University of Chicago Press, 1969), 102.

29. Perkins, *Film as Film*, 94.

30. Bill Nichols, ed., *Movies and Methods*, vol. 1 (Berkeley: University of California Press, 1976), 251, 401; Sam Rohdie, "Review: *Movie Reader*, *Film as Film*," *Screen* 13, no. 4 (1972): 143.

31. Perkins, *Film as Film*, 69.

32. Perkins, 121.

33. Perkins, 69.

34. Perkins, 83.

35. Perkins, 103–5.

36. Perkins, 94.

37. V. F. Perkins, "Rope," *Movie*, no. 7 (1963): 12; italics in original.

38. Perkins, 12.

39. Perkins, *Film as Film*, 120, 132.

40. V. F. Perkins, "The Cinema of Nicholas Ray," *Movie*, no. 9 (1963): 6.

41. V. F. Perkins, "*River of No Return*," *Movie*, no. 2 (1962): 19.

42. Perkins, *Film as Film*, 80–81.

43. V. F. Perkins quoted in Crouse, "Fueled by Enthusiasms," 23.

44. Perkins, *Film as Film*, 131.

45. Ian Cameron, "Films, Directors and Critics," *Movie*, no. 2 (1962): 4–7; also the note at the end of Ian Cameron, "Antonioni," *Film Quarterly* 16, no. 1 (1962): 58; and Gibbs, *The Life of Mise-en-Scène*, 97.

46. R. G. Collingwood, *The Principles of Art* (1938; repr., New York: Oxford University Press, 1958), 135–38; R. G. Collingwood, *The Idea of History*, rev. ed. (1946; repr., Oxford: Oxford University Press, 1994), 240–41.

47. Richard Dyer, personal communication, November 22, 2017.

48. V. F. Perkins, personal communication, February 8, 2016. This is from a draft of "Omission and Oversight in Close Reading" later cut from the published version.

49. V. F. Perkins, "Omission and Oversight in Close Reading: The Final Moments of Frederick Wiseman's High School," in *The Philosophy of Documentary Film: Image, Sound, Fiction, Truth*, ed. David LaRocca (Lanham, MD: Lexington Books, 2017), 392.

50. Perkins, *Film as Film*, 131–32.

51. Perkins, "*Letter from an Unknown Woman*," *Movie*, nos. 29–30 (1982): 61.

52. Perkins, 61.

53. Perkins, 67.
54. Perkins, 64.
55. Perkins, 68–69.

Coda

1. Maurice Merleau-Ponty, "The Film and the New Psychology," *Sense and Non-Sense*, trans. Hubert L. Dreyfus and Patricia Allen Dreyfus (Evanston, IL: Northwestern University Press, 1964), 53.

2. Merleau-Ponty, "The Film and the New Psychology," 59.

3. Christian Metz, *Film Language: A Semiotics of the Cinema*, trans. Michael Taylor (1968; repr., Chicago: University of Chicago Press, 1991), 42–43; Dudley Andrew, *André Bazin* (1978; repr., New York: Columbia University Press, 1990), chaps. 1 and 4.

4. André Bazin, *Jean Renoir*, trans. W. W. Halsey II and William H. Simon (New York: Dell, 1973), 86.

5. André Bazin, *What is Cinema?*, vol. 2, trans. Hugh Grayson (Berkeley: University of California Press, 1971), 37.

6. D. N. Rodowick, *The Virtual Life of Film* (Cambridge, MA: Harvard University Press, 2007), 117.

7. I borrow this phrase from Philip Rosen, *Change Mummified: Cinema, Historicity, Theory* (Minneapolis: University of Minnesota Press, 2001), 319ff.

8. Rodowick, *The Virtual Life of Film*, 123; René Descartes, quoted in Hans Jonas, *The Phenomenon of Life: Toward a Philosophical Biology* (1966; repr., Chicago: University of Chicago Press, 1982), 203.

9. Rodowick, *The Virtual Life of Film*, 118.

10. Scott Balcerzak, "Andy Serkis as Actor, Body and Gorilla: Motion Capture and the Presence of Performance," in *Cinephilia in the Age of Digital Reproduction: Film, Pleasure and Digital Culture, Vol. 1*, eds. Scott Balcerzak and Jason Sperb (London: Wallflower Press, 2009), 195–213; Tanine Allison, "More than a Man in a Monkey Suit: Andy Serkis, Motion Capture, and Digital Realism," *Quarterly Review of Film and Video* 28, no. 4 (2011): 325–41; and Lisa Bode, "Fleshing it Out: Prosthetic Makeup Effects, Motion Capture and the Reception of Performance," in *Special Effects: New Histories, Theories, Contexts*, eds. Dan North, Bob Rehak, and Michael Duffy (London: BFI-Palgrave, 2015), 32–44. For counterargument, see Sharon Marie Carnicke, "Emotional Expressivity in Motion Capture Technology," in *Acting and Performance in Moving Image Culture: Bodies, Screens, Renderings*, eds. Jörg Sternagel, Deborah Levitt, and Dieter Mersch (Bielefeld: Transcript Verlag, 2012), 17–34.

11. Lee Strasberg, *A Dream of Passion: The Development of the Method* (1987; repr., New York: Plume, 1988), 131.

12. Strasberg, *A Dream of Passion*, 132.

13. Strasberg, 150.

14. Isaac Butler, *The Method: How the Twentieth Century Learned to Act* (New York: Bloomsbury, 2022), 357–58.

15. Georg Henrik von Wright, *Explanation and Understanding* (Ithaca, NY: Cornell University Press, 1971), 47. See also Alexander Gerschenkron, *Continuity in History and Other Essays* (Cambridge, MA: Belknap, 1968), 11-39.

Bibliography

Archival Sources

Ray L. Birdwhistell Papers. Folklore Archives. Penn Museum.
Victor Oscar Freeburg Papers. Sterling Memorial Library. Yale University.
Wenner-Gren Foundation for Anthropological Research Files, New York.

Books and Articles

Alexander, Zeynep Çelik. *Kinaesthetic Knowing: Aesthetics, Epistemology, Modern Design*. Chicago: University of Chicago Press, 2017.

Allison, Tanine. "More than a Man in a Monkey Suit: Andy Serkis, Motion Capture, and Digital Realism." *Quarterly Review of Film and Video* 28, no. 4 (2011): 325–41.

Andrew, Dudley. *André Bazin*. New York: Columbia University Press, 1990. First published 1978.

Askari, Kaveh. *Making Movies into Art: Picture Craft From the Magic Lantern to Early Hollywood*. London: BFI-Palgrave, 2014.

Balcerzak, Scott. "Andy Serkis as Actor, Body and Gorilla: Motion Capture and the Presence of Performance." In *Cinephilia in the Age of Digital Reproduction: Film, Pleasure and Digital Culture, Vol. 1*, edited by Scott Balcerzak and Jason Sperb, 195–213. London: Wallflower Press, 2009.

Barker, Jennifer M. *The Tactile Eye: Touch and the Cinematic Experience*. Berkeley: University of California Press, 2009.

Barr, Charles. "CinemaScope: Before and After." *Film Quarterly* 16, no. 4 (1963): 4–24.

———. "Dolce Vita." *Granta* 64, no. 1207 (1961): 20.

———. "*The Entertainer*." *Granta* 64, no. 1202 (1960): 32–33.

Barrett, B. F. "The Photoplay Scenario: An Interview With Prof. Freeburg." *Motography*, November 11, 1916.

Basinger, Jeanine. *The Star Machine*. New York: Vintage, 2009.

Bates, Marston. *The Nature of Natural History*. Revised edition. New York: Scribner, 1961.

Bazin, André. *Jean Renoir*. Translated by W. W. Halsey II and William H. Simon. New York: Dell, 1973.

———. *What is Cinema? Volume 2*. Translated and edited by Hugh Gray. Berkeley: University of California Press, 1971.

Bierstedt, Robert. "Review: *Hollywood, the Dream Factory*." *American Sociological Review* 16, no. 1 (1951): 124–25.

Birdwhistell, Ray L. *Introduction to Kinesics: An Annotation System for Analysis of Body Motion and Gesture*. Washington, DC: U.S. Department of State, Foreign Service Institute, 1952.

———. "Kinesics." In *The Body Reader: Social Aspects of the Human Body*, edited by Ted Polhemus, 284–94. New York: Pantheon, 1978.

———. *Kinesics and Context: Essays on Body Motion Communication*. Philadelphia: University of Pennsylvania Press, 1970.

———. "The Language of the Body: The Natural Environment of Words." In *Human Communication: Theoretical Explorations*, edited by Albert Silverstein, 203–20. Hillsdale, NJ: Lawrence Erlbaum, 1974.

———. "Lecture at American Museum of Natural History, October 4, 1980." In McElvenny and Ploder, *Holisms of Communication*, 249–63. Berlin: Language Science Press, 2021.

———. "Training in Cultural Observation." *Human Organization Clearing-House Bulletin* 3, no. 3 (1955): 31–33.

———. "The Use of Audio-Visual Teaching Aids." In *Resources for the Teaching of Anthropology*, edited by David G. Mandelbaum, Gabriel W. Lasker, and Ethel M. Albert, 49–61. Berkeley: University of California Press, 1963.

Bode, Lisa. "Fleshing It Out: Prosthetic Makeup Effects, Motion Capture and the Reception of Performance." In *Special Effects: New Histories, Theories, Contexts*, edited by Dan North, Bob Rehak, and Michael Duffy, 32–44. London: BFI-Palgrave, 2015.

Bordwell, David. *Making Meaning: Inference and Rhetoric in the Interpretation of Cinema*. Cambridge, MA: Harvard University Press, 1989.

Boys, Barry. "*The Courtship of Eddie's Father*." *Movie*, no. 10 (1963): 29–32.

Butler, Isaac. *The Method: How the Twentieth Century Learned to Act*. New York: Bloomsbury, 2022.

Brewster, Ben, and Leah Jacobs. *Theatre to Cinema*. New York: Oxford University Press, 1997.

Byers, Paul. "A Personal View of Nonverbal Communication." *Theory into Practice* 16, no. 3 (1977): 134–40.

Cameron, Ian. "Against *This Sporting Life*" [unsigned]. *Movie*, no. 10 (1963): 21–22.

———. "Antonioni." *Film Quarterly* 16, no. 1 (1962): 1–58.

———. "Films, Directors and Critics." *Movie*, no. 2 (1962): 4–7.

Cameron, Ian, Paul Mayersberg, V. F. Perkins, and Mark Shivas. "*Movie* Differences." *Movie*, no. 8 (1963): 28–34.

Cameron, Ian, Paul Mayersberg, Vincente Minnelli, V. F. Perkins, and Mark Shivas. "Method: Vincente Minnelli." *Movie*, no. 1 (1962): 20–24.

Canetti, Elias. *The Memoirs of Elias Canetti*. Translated by Ralph Manheim and Joachim Neugroschel. New York: Farrar, Straus, and Giroux, 1999.

Capp, Al. *Li'l Abner: The Frazetta Years, Vol. 1, 1954–1955*. Edited by Denis Kitchen. Milwaukie, OR: Dark Horse Press, 2003.

Carnicke, Sharon Marie. "Emotional Expressivity in Motion Capture Technology." In *Acting and Performance in Moving Image Culture: Bodies, Screens, Renderings*, edited by Jörg Sternagel, Deborah Levitt, and Dieter Mersch, 17–34. Bielefeld: Transcript Verlag, 2012.

Cavell, Stanley. *The World Viewed: Reflections on the Ontology of Cinema*. Enlarged edition. Cambridge, MA: Harvard University Press, 1979.

Clark, Danae. *Negotiating Hollywood: The Cultural Politics of Actors' Labor*. Minneapolis: University of Minnesota Press, 1995.

Collingwood, R. G. *An Essay on Philosophical Method*. Oxford: Oxford University Press, 2005. First published 1933.

———. *The Idea of History*. Revised edition. Oxford: Oxford University Press, 1994. First published 1946.

———. *The Principles of Art*. New York: Oxford University Press, 1958. First published 1938.

Crouse, Jeffrey. "Fueled By Enthusiasms: Jeffrey Crouse Interviews V. F. Perkins." *Film International* 2, no. 3 (2004): 14–27.

Davis, Martha. "Film Projectors as Microscopes: Ray L. Birdwhistell and Microanalysis of Interaction (1955–1975)." *Visual Anthropology Review* 17, no. 2 (2001–2002): 39–49.

Decherney, Peter. *Hollywood and the Cultural Elite: How the Movies Became American*. New York: Columbia University Press, 2006.

deCordova, Richard. *Picture Personalities: The Emergence of the Star System in America*. Urbana: University of Illinois Press, 2001.

Dyer, Richard. "Four Films of Lana Turner." In *Star Texts: Image and Performance in Film and Television*, edited by Jeremy G. Butler, 214–27. Detroit, MI: Wayne State University Press, 1991.

"The Drews at Columbia." *Moving Picture World*, December 30, 1916.

Elsaesser, Thomas. "Tales of Sound and Fury: Observations on the Family Melodrama." *Monogram*, no. 4 (1972): 2–15.

Engelke, Henning. "Perception, Awareness, and Film Practice: A Natural History of the 'Doris Film.' " In McElvenny and Ploder, *Holisms of Communication*, 103–135.

"Flashes from the World of Cinema." *New York Sun*, July 15, 1917.

Ford, Ford Madox. *The Good Soldier: A Tale of Passion*. New York: Penguin, 1946. First published 1915.

Freeburg, Victor Oscar. *The Art of Photoplay Making*. New York: Macmillan, 1918.

———. "At My Window." *Los Angeles Herald*, November 16, 1909.

———. *Disguise Plots in Elizabethan Drama: A Study in Stage Tradition*. New York: Columbia University Press, 1915.

———. "'El Dorado' Rediscovered." *Forum* 73, no. 4 (1925): 474–89.

———. "Making America More American." *Swedish American Trade Journal* 15, no. 9 (1921): 332–34.

———. *Pictorial Beauty on the Screen*. New York: Macmillan, 1923.

"Freeburg, Victor Oscar." In *Who Was Who in American History: Arts and Letters*, 170. Chicago: Marquis Who's Who, 1975.

Fry, Roger. *Vision and Design*. London: Chatto and Windus, 1920.

Fur, Gunlög. *Painting Culture, Painting Nature: Stephen Mopope, Oscar Jacobson, and the Development of Indian Art in Oklahoma*. Norman: University of Oklahoma Press, 2019.

Gaboriau, Émile. *Monsieur Lecoq*. Translated by Laura E. Kendall. New York: Dover, 1975. First published 1869.

Gallagher, Catherine. "The Rise of Fictionality." In *The Novel, Volume 1: History, Geography, and Culture*, edited by Franco Moretti, 336–63. Princeton, NJ: Princeton University Press, 2006.

Geoghegan, Bernard Dionysius. "The Family as Machine: Film, Infrastructure, and Cybernetic Kinship in Suburban America." *Grey Room*, no. 66 (2017): 70–101.

Gerschenkron, Alexander. *Continuity in History and Other Essays*. Cambridge, MA: Belknap, 1968.

Gibbs, John. *The Life of Mise-en-Scène: Visual Style and British Film Criticism, 1946–1978*. Manchester, UK: Manchester University Press, 2013.

Golden, Herb. "Hollywood as 'Dream Factory' Just Nightmare to Femme Anthropologist." *Variety*, October 18, 1950.

Gottschalk, Louis A., and Arthur H. Auerbach, eds. *Methods of Research in Psychotherapy*. New York: Appleton-Century-Crofts, 1966.

Hamilton, Clayton. *The Art of Fiction: A Formulation of Its Fundamental Principles*. New York: Odyssey Press, 1939.

Hamilton, Walton H. "Institutions." In *Encyclopaedia of the Social Sciences*, vol. 8, 84–89. New York: Macmillan, 1949.

Hardy, Thomas. *Tess of the d'Urbervilles*. New York: Penguin, 1985. First published 1912.

Heath, Stephen. *Questions of Cinema*. Bloomington: Indiana University Press, 1981.

Heider, Karl G. *Ethnographic Film*. 2nd edition. Austin: University of Texas Press, 2006.

"Home-Made Motion Pictures Predicted for Near Future." *New York Times*, April 22, 1917.

Houseman, John. *Front and Center*. New York: Simon and Schuster, 1979.

Hoveyda, Fereydoun. "Nicholas Ray's Reply: *Party Girl*." Translated by Norman King. In *Cahiers du Cinéma: 1960s: New Wave, New Cinema, Reevaluating Hollywood*, edited by Jim Hillier, 122–31. Cambridge, MA: Harvard University Press, 1986.

"Howard Hawks." *Movie*, no. 5 (1962): 7

James, Henry. *The Portrait of a Lady*. New York: P. F. Collier and Son, 1917. First published 1881.

Joice, Katie. "Mothering in the Frame: Cinematic Microanalysis and the Pathogenic Mother, 1945–1967." *History of the Human Sciences* 34, no. 5 (2021): 105–31.

Jonas, Hans. *The Phenomenon of Life: Toward a Philosophical Biology*. Chicago: University of Chicago Press, 1982. First published 1966.

Kendon, Adam. "Some Theoretical and Methodological Aspects of the Use of Film in the Study of Social Interaction." In *Emerging Strategies in Social Psychological Research*, edited by G. P. Ginsburg, 67–91. London: Wiley, 1979.

Kendon, Adam, and Stuart J. Sigman. "Commemorative Essay: Ray L. Birdwhistell (1918–1994)." *Semiotica* 112, nos. 3–4 (1996): 239–46.

Koszarski, Richard. *An Evening's Entertainment: The Age of the Silent Feature Picture, 1915–1928*. New York: Charles Scribner's Sons, 1990.

———. "'It's No Use to Have an Unhappy Man': Paul Fejos at Universal." *Film History* 17, nos. 2–3 (2005): 234–40.

"Lana Turner Scrapbooks, 1939–1956." Performing Arts Library, New York. Microfilm.

"Lasky Company Offers Scholarship to Columbia Students." *Moving Picture World*, October 30, 1915.

Lawrence, D. H. *Sons and Lovers*. New York: Viking, 1958. First published 1913.

Lee, Vernon. *The Beautiful: An Introduction to Psychological Aesthetics*. Cambridge: Cambridge University Press, 1913.

Lee, Vernon, and C. Anstruther Thomson. "Beauty and Ugliness." In *Beauty and Ugliness and Other Studies in Psychological Aesthetics*, by Vernon Lee, 153–239. London: John Lane, 1912.

Leeds-Hurwitz, Wendy. "Notes in the History of Intercultural Communication: The Foreign Service Institute and the Mandate for Intercultural Training." *Quarterly Journal of Speech* 76, no. 3 (1990): 262–81.

Leeds-Hurwitz, Wendy, and Adam Kendon, "*The Natural History of an Interview* and the Microanalysis of Behavior in Social Interaction: A

Critical Moment in Research Practice." In McElvenny and Ploder, *Holisms of Communication*, 145–200. Berlin: Language Science Press, 2021.

Leeds-Hurwitz, Wendy, and Stuart J. Sigman. "The Penn Tradition." In *The Social History of Language and Social Interaction Research: People, Places, Ideas*, edited by Wendy Leeds-Hurwitz, 235–70. Cresskill, NJ: Hampton Press, 2010.

Liddell, Robert. *Robert Liddell on the Novel.* Chicago: University of Chicago Press, 1969.

"Life in Hollywood." *New Yorker*, March 5, 1949.

Lindsay, Vachel. *The Art of the Moving Picture*. New York: Modern Library, 2000. First published 1922.

———. *Letters of Vachel Lindsay*. Edited by Marc Chénetier. New York: Burt Franklin and Co., 1979.

Malinowski, Bronisław. "Culture." In *Encyclopaedia of the Social Sciences*, vol. 4, 621–45. New York: Macmillan, 1949.

———. *A Scientific Theory of Culture and Other Essays*. Chapel Hill: University of North Carolina Press, 1944.

Marks, Laura U. *The Skin of the Film: Intercultural Cinema, Embodiment, and the Senses*. Durham, NC: Duke University Press, 2000.

Martin, Adrian. "Available to Enjoyment (and Not Just in a Hedonistic Way): An Appreciation of Victor Perkins." Warwick Film and Television Studies. July 2016. https://warwick.ac.uk/fac/arts/film/archive/vfp/adrianmartin.

———. *Mise en Scène and Film Style: From Classical Hollywood to New Media Art*. London: Palgrave Macmillan, 2014.

McBride, Joseph. *Hawks on Hawks*. Lexington: University Press of Kentucky, 2013.

McDermott, Ray. "Profile: Ray L. Birdwhistell." *The Kinesis Report* 2, no. 3 (1980): 1–4, 14–16.

McElvenny, James, and Andrea Ploder, eds. *Holisms of Communication: The Early History of Audio-Visual Sequence Analysis*. Berlin: Language Science Press, 2021.

McLean, Adrienne L. "Feeling and the Filmed Body: Judy Garland and the Kinesics of Suffering." *Film Quarterly* 55, no. 3 (2002): 2–15.

McQuown, Norman, ed. *The Natural History of an Interview*. Chicago: University of Chicago Library, 1971. Microfilm.

Merleau-Ponty, Maurice. *Sense and Non-Sense*. Translated by Hubert L. Dreyfus and Patricia Allen Dreyfus. Evanston, IL: Northwestern University Press, 1964.

Metz, Christian. *Film Language: A Semiotics of the Cinema*. Translated by Michael Taylor. Chicago: University of Chicago Press, 1991. First published 1968.

Minnelli, Vincente. *I Remember It Well.* As told to Hector Arce. London: Angus and Robertson, 1975.

"Mr. Freeburg Receives Ph.D. From Columbia University." *Haverford News*, April 13, 1915.

Nichols, Bill, ed. *Movies and Methods, Vol. 1.* Berkeley: University of California Press, 1976.

Norris, Frank. *McTeague: A Story of San Francisco.* New York: Oxford University Press, 1995. First published 1899.

"October 16 Is Date Set by Lasky for Its Prize Play." *Motion Picture News*, October 21, 1916.

Ogden, C. K., and I. A. Richards. *The Meaning of Meaning.* San Diego: Harcourt Brace Jovanovich, 1989. First published 1923.

Perkins, V. F. "The British Cinema." *Movie*, no. 1 (1962): 2–7.

———. "Charm and Blood." *Oxford Opinion*, no. 42 (1960): 34–35.

———. "The Cinema of Nicholas Ray." *Movie*, no. 9 (1963): 4–10.

———. *Film as Film: Understanding and Judging Movies.* Harmondsworth, UK: Penguin, 1972.

———. "Ian Cameron: A Tribute." *Movie: A Journal of Film Criticism*, no. 1 (2010): 1–2.

———. "*King of Kings*." *Movie*, no. 1 (1962): 29–30.

———. "*Letter From an Unknown Woman*." *Movie*, nos. 29–30 (1982): 61–72.

———. "Nicholas Ray." *Oxford Opinion*, no. 40 (1960): 31–34.

———. "Omission and Oversight in Close Reading: The Final Moments of Frederick Wiseman's *High School*." In *The Philosophy of Documentary Film: Image, Sound, Fiction, Truth*, edited by David LaRocca, 381–94. Lanham, MD: Lexington Books, 2017.

———. "A Reply to Sam Rohdie." *Screen* 13, no. 4 (1972): 146–51.

———. "*River of No Return*." *Movie*, no. 2 (1962): 18–19.

———. "*Rope*." *Movie*, no. 7 (1963): 11–13.

———. "*Vivre sa Vie*." In *The Films of Jean-Luc Godard*, edited by Ian Cameron, 32–39. New York: Praeger, 1969.

———. "Where Is the World? The Horizon of Events in Movie Fiction." In *Style and Meaning: Studies in the Detailed Analysis of Film*, edited by John Gibbs and Douglas Pye, 16–41. Manchester, UK: Manchester University Press, 2005.

Perry, Bliss. *A Study of Prose Fiction.* Revised edition. Boston: Houghton Mifflin, 1920.

Polan, Dana. *Scenes of Instruction: The Beginnings of the U. S. Study of Film.* Berkeley: University of California Press, 2007.

Polhemus, Ted, ed. *The Body Reader: Social Aspects of the Human Body.* New York: Pantheon, 1978.

Powdermaker, Hortense. "An Anthropologist Looks at the Movies." *Annals of the American Academy of Political and Social Science*, no. 254 (1947): 80–87.

———. *Hollywood, the Dream Factory: An Anthropologist Looks at the Movie-makers*. Boston: Little, Brown, and Co., 1950.

———. *Life in Lesu: The Study of a Melanesian Society in New Ireland*. New York: Norton, 1971. First published 1933.

———. "Review: *Movies: A Psychological Study* by Martha Wolfenstein and Nathan Leites." *Psychiatry* 14, no. 3 (1951): 353–55.

———. *Stranger and Friend: The Way of an Anthropologist*. New York: Norton, 1966.

"Prof. Freeburg Sues for Share in Book." *Variety*, April 22, 1921.

"Prof's Next Pic Tome." *Variety*, December 20, 1950.

Ramsaye, Terry. "An Anthropologist Looks at Hollywood." *Motion Picture Herald*, October 14, 1950.

Richter, Hans. "The Badly Trained Sensibility." Translated by Mike Weaver. In *The Avant-Garde Film: A Reader of Theory and Criticism*, edited by P. Adams Sitney, 22–23. New York: Anthology Film Archives, 1987. First published in 1924.

Rodowick, D. N. *The Virtual Life of Film*. Cambridge, MA: Harvard University Press, 2007.

Rohdie, Sam. "Review: *Movie Reader*, *Film as Film*." *Screen* 13, no. 4 (1972): 135–45.

Rosen, Philip. *Change Mummified: Cinema, Historicity, Theory*. Minneapolis: University of Minnesota Press, 2001.

Ross, Lillian. "Picture." In *Reporting*, 223–442. New York: Dodd, Mead, and Co., 1981.

Sargent, Epes Winthrop. "Wanted—A Museum." *Moving Picture World*, September 9, 1916.

Scheflen, Albert E. *Communicational Structure: Analysis of a Psychotherapy Transaction*. Bloomington: Indiana University Press, 1973.

———. "Natural History Method in Psychotherapy: Communicational Research." In *Methods of Research in Psychotherapy*, edited by Louis A Gottschalk and Arthur H. Auerbach, 263–89. New York: Appleton-Century-Crofts, 1966.

Schiller, Friedrich. *On the Aesthetic Education of Man in a Series of Letters*. Translated by Reginald Snell. New Haven, CT: Yale University Press, 1954. First published 1795.

Schlesinger, Arthur M., Jr. "The Anthropological Fallacy." *The Nation*, December 30, 1950.

Schulberg, Budd. "Hollywood Primitive." *New York Times*, October 15, 1950.

Shaftesbury, Lord. *Characteristicks of Men, Manners, Opinions, Times*. Indianapolis, IN: Liberty Fund, 2001. First published 1711.

Shaviro, Steven. *The Cinematic Body*. Minneapolis: University of Minnesota Press, 1993.

Shivas, Mark. "Minnelli's Method." *Movie*, no. 1 (1962): 17–19.

———. "New Approach." *Movie*, no. 8 (1963): 13–15.

Sklar, Robert. *City Boys: Cagney, Bogart, Garfield*. Princeton, NJ: Princeton University Press, 1992.

Sobchack, Vivian. *The Address of the Eye: A Phenomenology of Film Experience*. Princeton, NJ: Princeton University Press, 1990.

Sperber, A. M., and Eric Lax. *Bogart*. New York: William Morrow and Co., 1997.

Staiger, Janet. *Interpreting Films: Studies in the Historical Reception of American Cinema*. Princeton, NJ: Princeton University Press, 1992.

Strasberg, Lee. *A Dream of Passion: The Development of the Method*. New York: Plume, 1988.

"Taking the Movies to College at Columbia University." *New York Tribune*, August 10, 1919.

Tsivian, Yuri. "Some Historical Footnotes to the Kuleshov Experiment." Translated by Kathy Porter. In *Early Cinema: Space, Frame, Narrative*, edited by Thomas Elsaesser, 249–50. London: BFI, 1990.

"True Purposes of Columbia's Course in 'Movie' Play Writing." *New York Sun*, October 17, 1915.

Turner, Lana. *Lana: The Lady, the Legend, the Truth*. New York: E. P. Dutton, 1982.

Uzzell, Thomas H. *Narrative Technique: A Practical Course in Literary Psychology*. New York: Harcourt, Brace, and Co., 1924.

Valentino, Lou. *The Films of Lana Turner*. Secaucus, NJ: Citadel Press, 1976.

Van Vlack, Jacques D. "Filming Psychotherapy from the Viewpoint of a Research Cinematographer." In *Methods of Research in Psychotherapy*, edited by Louis A Gottschalk and Arthur H. Auerbach, 13–24. New York: Appleton-Century-Crofts, 1966.

———. "The Research Document Film." *American Science Film Association Notes* 1, no. 5 (1965): 9–11.

Watt, Ian. *The Rise of the Novel*. Berkeley: University of California Press, 2001. First published 1957.

Weinstein, Deborah. *The Pathological Family: Postwar America and the Rise of Family Therapy*. Ithaca, NY: Cornell University Press, 2013.

Williams, Linda. "Film Bodies: Gender, Genre, and Excess." *Film Quarterly* 44, no. 4 (1991): 2–13.

Wolf, Eric R. "Hortense Powdermaker 1900–1970." *American Anthropologist* 73, no. 3 (1971): 783–86.

Wood, Robin. "Attitudes in *Advise and Consent*." *Movie*, no. 4 (1962): 14–17.

Woolf, Virginia. *Roger Fry*. New York: Mariner, 1976. First published 1940.

Wright, Georg Henrik von. *Explanation and Understanding*. Ithaca, NY: Cornell University Press, 1971.

Index

www.ingramcontent.com/pod-product-compliance
Lightning Source LLC
LaVergne TN
LVHW010348080826
844660LV00003B/219

* 9 7 8 1 4 3 8 4 9 5 0 8 8 *